AutoCAD 2013
for the Interior Designer

Dean Muccio

ISBN: 978-1-58503-715-5

D1307859

PUBLICATIONS

Schroff Development Corporation

www.SDCpublications.com

SDC Publications
P.O. Box 1334
Mission KS 66222
(913) 262-2664
www.SDCpublications.com

Publisher: Stephen Schroff

Acknowledgements

This 2013 version emphasizes the AutoCAD® 2D Drafting and Annotation Workspace. Previous versions had focused on the AutoCAD® Classic Workspace; however, multiple requests had prompted the change.

I would like to thank my family, and especially my beautiful wife Mary, for encouraging me and for having the patience with the many hours that were spent on the original project, and this update.

About the Author

Dean Muccio is an adjunct Assistant Professor at Fairfield University in Fairfield, CT, and has been teaching since the late 1980's. He has taught a variety of Engineering Graphics and Computer Aided Design and Manufacturing courses, and for the past several years, has taught AutoCAD® for the Interior Design program.

In addition to teaching part-time, Dean is a full-time Engineering Manager at Sikorsky Aircraft Corporation in Stratford, CT. He holds a B.S. degree in Mechanical Engineering from Norwich University, and an M.S. degree in Mechanical Engineering from Yale University.

Dean is a DIY homeowner who has tackled many remodeling projects. He has applied his engineering knowledge to refine his woodworking skills and to develop creative design solutions for space planning. The remodeling projects have provided a practical insight into what an Interior Designer must deal with when creating a design.

Notes:

Table of Contents

Index

Chapter 1
Getting Comfortable with AutoCAD®

Learning Objectives:

- **Going from drafting to CAD – Ground rules of using AutoCAD®**
- **Getting familiar with the AutoCAD® Workspace screens**
- **Understanding AutoCAD® Toolbars**
- **Getting AutoCAD® Help**
- **Customizing your screen appearance and right mouse button**
- **Using a Flash Drive**
- **Opening and Saving drawings**

Introduction to AutoCAD®

Congratulations on your decision to use the computer to draw your interior designs. AutoCAD® is an excellent product that is very popular. Having your designs in AutoCAD® format allows you to make changes easier, and also allows you to integrate your interior design with the architect's design. In fact, if an architectural drawing is already available on AutoCAD®, you can use that to build upon for your interior design.

There are many advantages to using AutoCAD® instead of drawing by hand:

- Drawings are done full size and scaled only for printing.
- Working with a design team is easier with AutoCAD®.
- You draw fixtures, furniture, appliances, etc. only one time and re-use them for other drawings.
- You can use items drawn by other designers; you no longer need to trace.
- You can have a library of items for re-use.
- You can use layers to visualize select items at a time.
- You can create/erase construction lines, etc. without the mess.

A major advantage to using AutoCAD® is that all your drawings are done in full scale. For example, if the measurements of the room you are designing are 20′ x 20′, you actually draw the room as 20′ x 20′. If you have been doing your drawings by hand, you have been drawing to scale. Perhaps you have been drawing to ¼″ = 1′. This required you to use an architect scale or a calculator. You do not have to use either of these when drawing on AutoCAD®.

Not only does this save you time, but it also makes integrating other drawings into your design very simple. Since it is standard practice to do drawings full scale on AutoCAD®, the architectural drawing, and any available drawings such as furniture, appliances, etc. are readily available for your use. Sharing your designs with other designers and vice versa is made easy by drawing to full scale. In fact, there are several Internet sites that have pre-drawn AutoCAD® items such as furniture, plants, appliances, etc. Some are available for free; others are available for a small charge.

The AutoCAD® LT version is for 2D drafting, and it is all the Interior Designer needs to complete floor plan and elevation type drawings. It is more economical than buying the complete AutoCAD® version, which includes 3D. Either version works the same in the 2D mode (there is some advanced functionality that is not included in the LT version, but is not a necessity for the Interior Designer).

The AutoCAD® program has been upgraded over the years to include many enhancements. Since the AutoCAD® 2004 version, most improvements were in the appearance of some command dialog boxes, and right mouse-click functionality. As of this writing, the latest version is AutoCAD® 2013. For the most part, the instructions within this text can be used for versions 2004 through 2013. There may be some differences in the look of things, but the same basic procedures and functions have remained the same. The designer can easily adapt to these differences without the need for a completely new course or text.

Hand Drawing vs. AutoCAD®

Using the computer to create your drawings may seem intimidating. This may be true especially if have not done it before and only use a computer for e-mail, family photos, and shopping. Perhaps you have used it to touch up some photographs using one of the many programs available.

You may be surprised at first that AutoCAD® does not treat drawings the same as touching up photos. That is because AutoCAD® recognizes the items on your drawing screen as specific objects such as lines, circles, arcs, etc. This is similar to how a word processing program recognizes the characters on the screen as letters, numbers, etc. – especially when you are using a spellchecker.

When you create your designs using drafting techniques, you strive for accuracy. This is necessary because items must fit properly. It can be discouraging (and expensive) when the carpenter tells you that the cabinets don't fit properly (or any other item) and to make up for it you have to revise the design. Had your measurements and drafting been accurate in the first place, this mistake could have been avoided. Although AutoCAD® cannot help you in measuring your client's rooms correctly, once you have the measurements, they are accurately reflected on the computer.

Accuracy in AutoCAD® is achieved by the fact that it uses X and Y coordinates to determine exactly where lines, circles, arcs, etc. are on the drawing. Fortunately, we do not have to burden ourselves with this fact, and we can create our designs in confidence knowing that AutoCAD® is working to keep it precise.

Throughout this book, we will do our best to avoid using X and Y coordinates. Instead, the intention is to keep the method of drawing as similar as possible to how you are currently creating drawings using your drafting equipment.

For example:

- We will draw lines longer than needed and trim them as required
  - o Trimming will be like using your erasing shield to remove the excess line and have a clean intersection
- We will use circles and trim them to become arcs
  - o Just like when you use a circle template or compass, sometimes you draw an arc bigger than needed and have to clean it up with your erasing shield

The best part is that we will not have eraser debris all over the place!

Clarifications and Ground Rules

Before we begin, it is best to clarify how to interact with the computer so that AutoCAD® interprets your intentions correctly. Because it is a computer, it is looking at specific ways in which you communicate with it. You will be primarily using your mouse to pick locations on your drawing and selecting commands via icons or pull-down menus. You will also use your keyboard to key in specific values, and also for command shortcuts.

The following may help you throughout this book and with using AutoCAD®. Some of the rules will be needed as we progress, so you may wish to refer back to them, as we get further along.

Clarifications:

1. The words Pick, or Select, are meant to indicate that you must use your mouse/cursor and left click. For instances where a right mouse click is needed, it will be specifically stated to right-click.
2. Whenever it is required to type in a value or option letter, this must be followed by pressing the ↵ Enter key. AutoCAD® will not recognize what you have typed on the command line until the ↵ Enter key is pressed.

AutoCAD® Ground Rules:

1. AutoCAD® is based on an X-Y coordinate system. The horizontal direction, starting from left and going right, is the positive X direction. Starting from right and going left is the negative X direction. The vertical direction, starting from the bottom of the screen and moving up, is the positive Y direction. Starting from the top of the screen and moving down is the negative Y direction. This book will attempt to avoid referring to X and Y directions; instead, it will refer to horizontal and vertical directions.

2. Positive angles are measured by starting from the positive X-axis and rotating in a counterclockwise direction. Note that you can use negative angles. For example, -90° is the same as 270°.

Angles are measured counterclockwise

3. To exit a command, press the ↵ Enter key or space bar. The Escape key (Esc) can also be used, but sometimes the Escape key will not work (depending on the command).
4. To repeat the previous command you used, press the ↵ Enter key. This comes in handy for fillets and offsets.
5. The default measurement is inches. When keying in distance values for feet, remember to use the foot symbol.
6. Standard practice is to draw everything full scale.
7. If you select objects with no command in the command line, AutoCAD® will show grips on that object (little blue boxes). Grips can be removed by pressing the Escape key.

The AutoCAD® Screen

To help guide you through learning AutoCAD®, it is a good idea to get familiar with the AutoCAD® screen. Various toolbars, menus, and screen areas are mentioned throughout this text. The following figure will help you get familiar with the names of these items.

Application Menu Browser – Pull-down Menu Items can be accessed using this

The Ribbon Tabs – Each tab is used to select a toolbar by group

Quick Access Toolbar – Contains frequently used Windows icons for files

The Ribbon – Contains Panels which are a style of toolbars tabulated by group

Drawing Area

Command Line

Status Bar

Workspace Switching icon

Default 2D Drafting & Annotation AutoCAD® screen

The default AutoCAD® screen is the 2D Drafting & Annotation screen. This can be changed to the AutoCAD® Classic screen by using the Workspace Switching icon found on the lower right side of the status bar.

Pull-down menus are available on the screen – No need to use the menu browser.

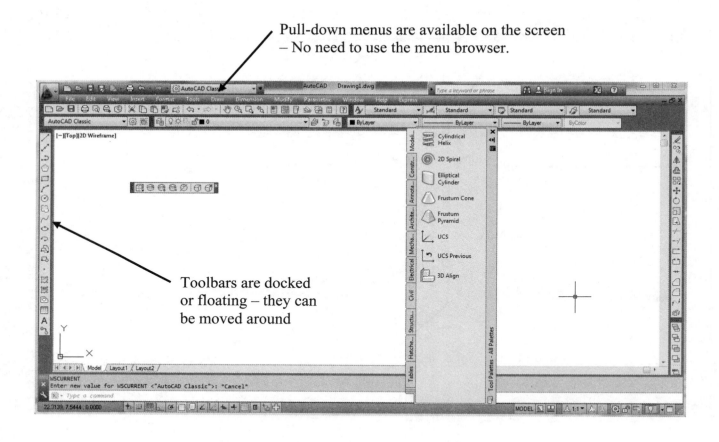

AutoCAD® Classic screen

Status Bar icons

Before we begin drawing, let's turn off the icons on the status bar. These are like switches – left click once to turn on, left click again to turn off. When they are turned on, they appear blue, when off, they are gray. The only icon to leave on is the Object Snap. We will discuss this more in later chapters.

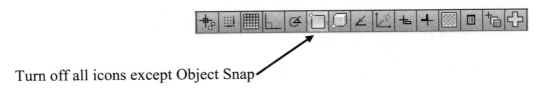

Turn off all icons except Object Snap

Toolbars

AutoCAD® has numerous toolbars, but not all toolbars are shown on your screen. Toolbars can be used via the Ribbon (for the 2D Drafting and Annotation workspace), or can be brought up individually.

AutoCAD® Classic

To bring up an individual toolbar, pick on the Pull-Down Menu and select Tools, then Toolbars, then AutoCAD®. Choose your desired toolbar from the list.

An easier way to bring up additional toolbars that are not currently shown on the screen is to right-click on any toolbar. This will bring up a list of available toolbars. Some items on the list will have a checkmark in front of them. Those are the ones that are currently on the screen.

In order to display an additional toolbar, move the cursor over the name of the toolbar you want and pick it.

As an example, let's bring up the Inquiry toolbar. Move the cursor over the list of toolbars until Inquiry is highlighted. Pick (left-click) on the word Inquiry. An Inquiry toolbar will appear on the drawing screen and the list of toolbars will disappear.

When the toolbar appears on the drawing space it is considered a "floating" toolbar. When it is off to the side it is "docked".

The floating toolbar can be moved around the drawing screen by picking it on the end bar portion and dragging it to a new location. If you drag it close enough to any of the four edges of the drawing screen, the outline of the toolbar will change orientation to vertical or remain horizontal – depending on which edge you dock it to. This indicates that it will dock to that edge if you let go of the mouse button. You can move a docked toolbar by picking the end bar portion and dragging it to a new location.

To turn off a toolbar, you can right click on any toolbar and pick the toolbar that you want to turn off from the list of toolbars. The toolbar that you want to turn off must already be turned on. This is indicated by the check mark in front of it on the list. If you want to turn off a floating toolbar, you can simply pick the "X" on the upper right portion of the bar.

AutoCAD® allows the flexibility to relocate docked toolbars. This is a personal preference. Many designers prefer to have the modify toolbar next to the draw toolbar. Some designers prefer to have those toolbars on the right side of the screen instead of the left side. It does not matter where the toolbars are located, they will still work.

2D Drafting and Annotation

The Ribbon also contains similar toolbars that the Classic workspace offers. It is simply a different option of accessing the AutoCAD® commands.

Tools are categorized by function and are accessed by selecting each tab. Each tab contains Panels. The Home tab contains the basic commands and will be the most used tab. This text will utilize the 2D Drafting and Annotation workspace.

Command Line

AutoCAD® utilizes a command line to display which command is selected and to prompt the designer for additional steps needed to complete the command. The command line is located near the bottom of the drawing space screen.

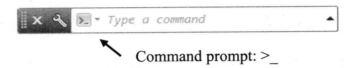

Command prompt: >_

The command line can be relocated on the screen by dragging from the left edge. It can also be re-sized by moving your cursor near the right edge of the outline until it changes to a split-arrow cursor. Select the right edge and drag right or left to re-size the command line.

When a command is selected, AutoCAD® automatically enters the command text into the command line. When applicable, the command icon is also displayed in the command line, replacing the command prompt.

The following will appear in the command line when the LINE command is selected:

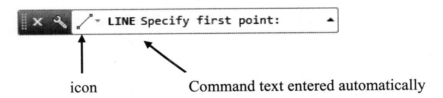

icon   Command text entered automatically

Commands can be entered directly into the command line if desired. Some commands have "hot keys" that will allow a single character to represent the whole command. This saves typing.

During the command, you may be prompted for additional information or action. Each time the command line changes information, the previous text is displayed above the outline. Up to three lines are displayed with transparent text that will disappear from the screen after several seconds.

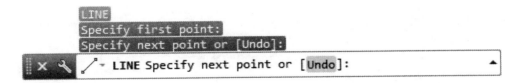

A longer list of previously displayed command line text can be viewed by selecting the up-arrow on the right-hand side of the outline.

Options – Screen Color & Right-Click

When you start up AutoCAD® 2013 for the first time, you will notice that the background is black with white gridlines. If you like this look, then you won't need to review this section. If you would like to change the background to a different color, such as white, then the following information will help you achieve that.

Customizing Screen Background Color

To change your drawing space background color, pick the Application Menu Browser button at the top-left of the screen and select Options.

The Options dialog box will pop up. Make sure the Display tab near the top of the dialog box is selected. Select the Colors button.

The Drawing Window Colors dialog box pops up. Use the pull down selection for 2D model space. Change the color of the Uniform background to White by using the pull-down selection under Color. If you plan to change other colors, the color changes need to be done for each Interface element individually.

When done, select Apply & Close button. Pick the OK button to close the Options dialog box.

After you exit the dialog box, you will now have a white screen background. Of course, if you prefer a different color, the steps to make the changes are the same as described.

Customizing Right-Click

The default setting for AutoCAD® Right-Click (in the drawing space) is to bring up the shortcut menu. Since repeating the previous command by pressing the ↵ Enter key requires a keyboard operation, it can be more convenient to use the right mouse button to repeat the previous command instead.

Shortcut menu is default setting

To repeat the previous command (for this example the previous command was Circle), highlight and either left or right click.

The function of the right mouse button can be customized by using Options. Pick the User Preferences tab near the top of the dialog box. Select the Right-click Customization button.

The Right-Click Customization dialog box pops up. Pick to place a checkmark to turn on time-sensitive right-click. When done, select the Apply & Close button. Pick the OK button to close the Options dialog box.

This option allows you to use the right mouse button to repeat the last command without bringing up the shortcut menu, unless you press and hold the button for longer period of time.

UCS icon, Navigation Bar and View Cube

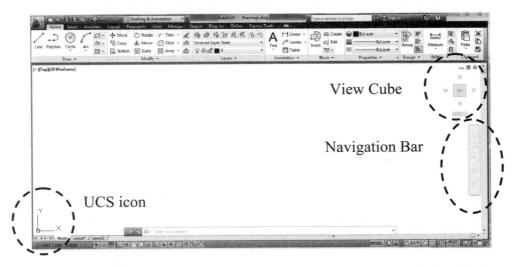

Additional display changes you may desire to make are to eliminate the X-Y axis (which is called the UCS icon), the Navigation Bar, and the View Cube. You eliminate the View Cube and Navigation Bar by using the User Interface pull-down menu, found on the User Interface Panel in the View Tab on the Ribbon, and un-checking the check-boxes for each.

To eliminate the UCS icon, pick the fly-out arrow on the User Interface Panel (shown circled above). This will bring up the same Options dialog box we had before. Pick the 3D Modeling tab and un-check the check-boxes for both items under the "Display the UCS Icon" section of the dialog box.

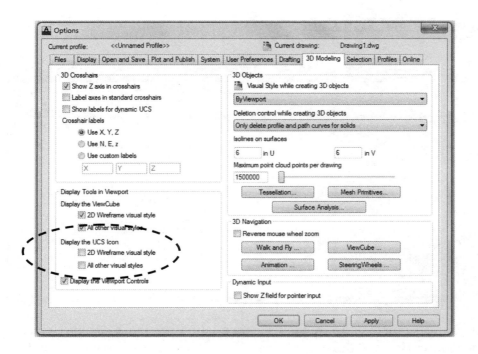

AutoCAD® Help

The intention of this book is not to cover every command in complete detail. Instead, it will provide enough information for the new user to be productive using AutoCAD® as quickly as possible. There are some textbooks available that attempt to provide a comprehensive instructional guide on how to use AutoCAD®, and in those, there may still be some things that are not covered. You can refer to other texts if you may be seeking a different explanation of how a command works. Or, as an alternative, you can use the Help feature within the program. Fortunately, AutoCAD® has provided a very good Help menu, which can be searched by topic. Like most other AutoCAD® functions, there are several ways to access the Help screen. You can use the Help icon or pull-down, or simply press the F1 key.

Using any of these methods will get you to the Help screen. You can explore commands and additional features. It is user-friendly, and self-explanatory. When you want to check features in more detail, this is the best way to do that.

Using a Flash Drive

A Flash Drive (other names for this include: jump drive, removable disk, travel drive, USB mass storage device, thumb drive etc.) comes in handy when you want to transport your drawings or documents from one computer to another. This is a very convenient method, as opposed to e-mailing them or burning the information to a CD, or a floppy disk. Most modern computers do not have floppy disk drives anymore, and not all computers have the ability to write to a CD. However, most modern computers have a USB port.

USB Ports on
the computer

Flash Drive
Other names: jump drive, removable disk,
travel drive, USB mass storage device, etc.

Flash drives come in different shapes, sizes, and colors. They also come in different memory capacity ranging from 128 MB to 4 GB and larger. As with most electronic items, prices come down and memory capacity goes up over time. These are typically on sale every week at any office product store, computer store, or other electronic store, including large retailers that sell electronics.

Saving your drawings to the flash drive is very similar to saving them in the My Documents folder on the C: drive (or D: drive if your computer has been set up that way). Prior to saving your drawing, make sure the flash drive is plugged into the USB port on the computer. It may take a minute (more or less) for your computer to recognize the flash drive, and you may get a message in your Windows Tray (on the lower part of the screen) indicating that the new USB Mass Storage Device was detected. If a dialog box opens up, close it out.

Once the flash drive is installed, simply use "Save As…" in the File pull-down menu. A dialog box will appear. Use the pull-down arrow to select the "Save in" location for your drawing.

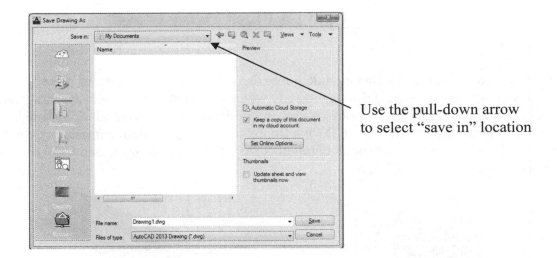

Use the pull-down arrow
to select "save in" location

Pick the USB Disk. Note that the drive letter is automatically assigned by your computer. It will use the next available drive letter. In this example the drive letter assigned is (D:).

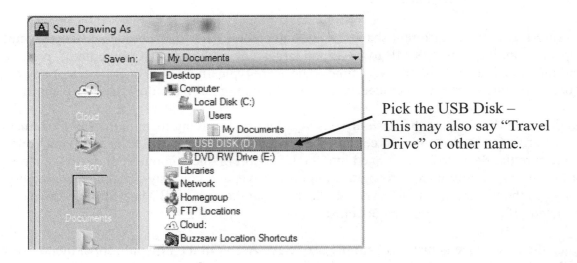

Pick the USB Disk –
This may also say "Travel
Drive" or other name.

The "Save in" location is now the USB Disk. You can rename your drawing if you wish as shown:

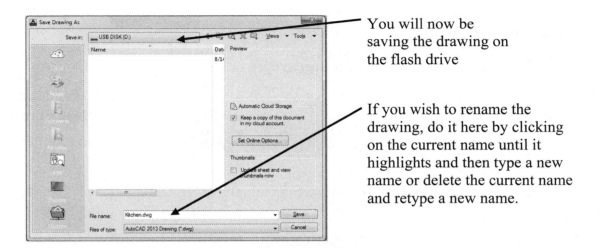

You will now be saving the drawing on the flash drive

If you wish to rename the drawing, do it here by clicking on the current name until it highlights and then type a new name or delete the current name and retype a new name.

You can also change the file type to accommodate older versions of AutoCAD® (*.dwg) or other PC based CAD system using Drawing Exchange Format (*.dxf). Or you can save this as a template file (*.dwt), which is typically used for drawing formats. Use the pull-down arrow for "Files of type:" to choose the type of file you wish to save this as:

Pick the Save button when all selections are complete

Once all selections have been made, pick the Save button and the drawing will be saved to the flash drive.

Recommendation: Don't forget to take you Flash Drive out when done! Because this is so small it is easy to forget it or lose it. It is a good idea to make a back-up copy (periodically) of your Flash Drive. In the event that it does get lost, at least you will not lose all your work.

Opening and Saving Drawings

Before beginning, it is recommended that you understand how to save your work. In addition, knowing how to manage files using Windows is very helpful. If you already know how to do that, this section will be a review for you.

Using Pull-Down Menu

You can use the Application Menu Browser to open or save your drawing.

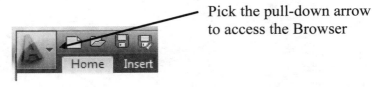

Pick the pull-down arrow
to access the Browser

The following selections will be the ones we are initially interested in:

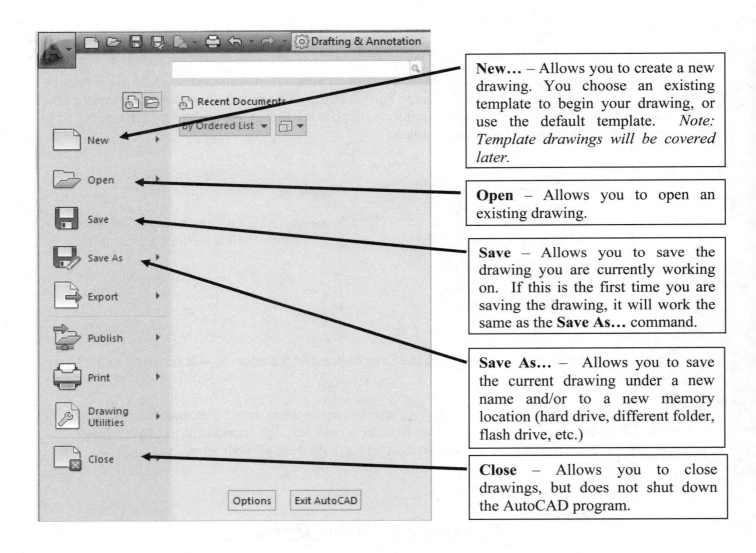

New... – Allows you to create a new drawing. You choose an existing template to begin your drawing, or use the default template. *Note: Template drawings will be covered later.*

Open – Allows you to open an existing drawing.

Save – Allows you to save the drawing you are currently working on. If this is the first time you are saving the drawing, it will work the same as the **Save As...** command.

Save As... – Allows you to save the current drawing under a new name and/or to a new memory location (hard drive, different folder, flash drive, etc.)

Close – Allows you to close drawings, but does not shut down the AutoCAD program.

Selecting New...

When you select the New... option, AutoCAD® displays a Select template dialog box. The default location that it will look in is the template folder which is part of the AutoCAD® software package installed on the computer. AutoCAD® will pre-select a default template, which is a blank drawing. Otherwise, you can choose many of the other available templates. You can scroll through the list to see the many templates AutoCAD® already has available to you. You can highlight (single left-click) any of them. As you do so, the Preview pane in the upper right side of the dialog box will show you a thumbnail view of the template.

Once you determine which template drawing you wish to use, either double-left-click on that template, or, once that template is highlighted, pick the Open button.

Template drawings are helpful in that you start with a drawing that has all the customization included. For example, the drawing border and title block can already be included in the template. Later, you will learn how to create your own template drawing.

Look in: shows you which folder you are looking for the template

Using Pull-Down arrow allows you to choose the folder to look in

Icons allow you to create a new folder or go up a folder, etc.

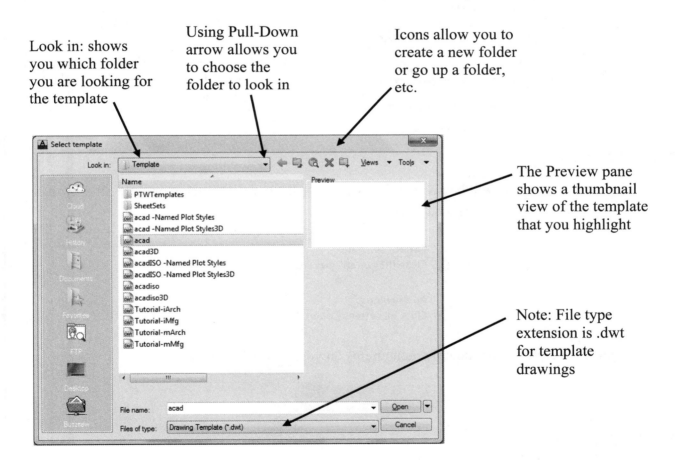

The Preview pane shows a thumbnail view of the template that you highlight

Note: File type extension is .dwt for template drawings

Selecting Open

Selecting Open is very similar to selecting New… because AutoCAD® will be looking for an existing drawing. But instead of looking for a template drawing, which has a .dwt file extension, it will be looking for an AutoCAD® drawing with a .dwg file extension. You can change the file type extension that you wish to open by using the pull-down arrow in the "Files of type:" box.

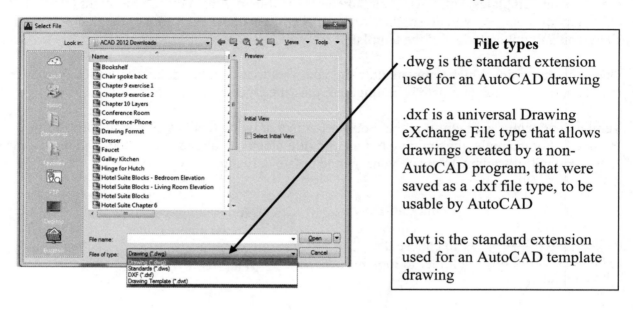

File types

.dwg is the standard extension used for an AutoCAD drawing

.dxf is a universal Drawing eXchange File type that allows drawings created by a non-AutoCAD program, that were saved as a .dxf file type, to be usable by AutoCAD

.dwt is the standard extension used for an AutoCAD template drawing

Selecting Close

When you select Close, you will be given a choice to close the current drawing or close all drawings.

Close the drawing

Current Drawing
Close the current drawing.

All Drawings
Close all currently open drawings.

If all drawings are closed, then the only menu items on your screen are these:

Selecting Save

When you select **Save**, a dialog box will appear if this is the first time you are saving your drawing, and the command works the same as the **Save As…** command. This is because a new drawing is given a default name by AutoCAD®, such as Drawing1.dwg, and it is likely you would not want to save it under that name.

If this is not the first time saving the drawing, selecting **Save** will replace the existing version that was saved previously with the current version. In that case, no dialog box will appear, but the command line will show _qsave. This is what AutoCAD® refers to as a Quick Save.

Selecting Save As...

Use Save As... to save your drawing under a new name or to save it in a different location. This is useful if you wish to modify a drawing, but still want to preserve the original version. It is also useful if you want to save a duplicate copy to a separate folder or to a Flash Drive.

A Save As... dialog box will appear when this is chosen.

File types

You can choose to save your drawing as the current or earlier version of AutoCAD® as a .dwg, .dwt, or .dxf. We will be primarily saving our drawings as a .dwg type. In later chapters, we will create our own template, which is a .dwt type. We will not be using the .dxf type. This type is used to enable other non-AutoCAD® programs to read an AutoCAD® drawing.

Saving your drawing as an earlier version allows sharing your files with other AutoCAD® users that are using an older version of AutoCAD®

Look in:/Save in: & Icons

The "Look in:" or "Save in:" work the same way. Understanding where your drawing is being saved, or where the drawing is located so that you can open it, is very important. You want to be able to locate your drawing later to make changes, etc. The pull-down arrow and the Icons help you manage that. A more detailed explanation can be found in File Management.

Summary

The topics covered in this chapter are meant to be an introduction to the AutoCAD® working environment. It is meant to help you feel more comfortable creating drawings on the computer. When you have completed this chapter, you should now have an understanding of the following:

- Differences between drawing by hand vs. using AutoCAD®
- Different ways of selecting AutoCAD® commands
- The different AutoCAD® Workspaces available
- Toolbars – how to bring them up and dock them for AutoCAD® Classic workspace
- Using the Help feature
- Customize your screen colors and your right mouse button
- Using a Flash Drive
- Opening, and saving your drawings

Review Questions

1. What are the advantages of using AutoCAD® instead of drawing by hand?

2. Why do you always draw full scale in AutoCAD®?

3. Which direction are angles measured in AutoCAD®?

4. What are the different Workspaces called that you can work in?

5. How can you bring up a different toolbar in AutoCAD® Classic workspace?

6. How do you access the Help feature?

7. Which pull-down menu and option do you use to change the screen color and customize the right mouse button?

8. What is a Flash Drive, how do you use it, what other names describe it?

9. How do you open and save AutoCAD® drawings?

10. Why would you want to save your drawing as an earlier version of AutoCAD®?

Chapter 2
Setting-up and Intro to AutoCAD®

Learning Objectives:

- **Changing from Decimal to Architectural Units**
- **Three basic commands to get started**
    - Line
    - Circle
    - Erase
- **Methods of selecting objects**
- **Getting around your drawing by using Zoom and Pan**

Units

The Units command allows you to set the unit of measure for your drawing. For Interior Design, we want units of Feet and Inches. AutoCAD® names this style of units Architectural. The default style is Decimal, with a precision of 4 decimal places, so you will need to change it to Architectural.

Procedure:

Pick (left click): **Application Menu Browser,** select **Drawing Utilities,** and select **Units**

A dialog box will appear:

The dialog box contains pull-down selections for Length, Angle, and Insertion scale. We will not change the insertion scale. Within Length and Angle choices, there are also pull-down selections for Precision. Changing the precision only affects the displayed values of the coordinates and values shown when using Distance or List Commands (both to be discussed in later chapters). It does not change the true value of the object, which is stored in the AutoCAD® model at a very high precision.

4-Place, Decimal   1/16″, Architectural

X,Y, & Z Coordinate Values of the cursor location
are displayed in the selected precision and unit type

Change the units for Length to Architectural:

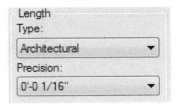

The Precision will automatically change to fraction style. Ensure that 1/16″ is the precision. If not, use the pull-down selection to change it.

Leave the default values for Angle at Decimal Degrees with 0 Precision, with the Clockwise check box unchecked. Note that the default direction for angles is counterclockwise. We will leave this alone.

Feel free to explore different styles and precisions. When you are done exploring, set the values to those shown in the above figure.

Three Easy Commands to Help Get You Started

Line

The Line command creates a point-to-point line. AutoCAD® allows you to create multiple end-to-end lines within the single command. The Line command is a very basic AutoCAD® command.

Procedure:

Pick (left click): **Line icon** from the Draw Panel of the Home Tab.

The command line prompts you with the following:

LINE Specify first point:

Pick anywhere on your screen to begin to draw a line.

After you specify the first point, the line will appear on the screen, anchored at the point you just picked, and will "rubber-band" to follow your cursor. The command line prompts you with the following:

Specify next point or [Undo]:

Left click on the screen again and a line will be created. A second line will start; anchored at the second point you just picked, and will "rubber-band" again to follow your cursor. Because AutoCAD® does not know how many lines you intend to draw, the command line will continue to prompt you with the following:

Specify next point or [Undo]:

When you are done drawing lines, press the ↵ Enter key to exit the Line command.

AutoCAD® will exit the Line command and display a command prompt.

Although other methods of putting lines on your drawing exist, they will not be covered here. You can explore these on your own using the help menu.

Recommendation:

The Line command has limited use. It is recommended to use this command when you want to draw lines between two existing points (such as endpoints of existing lines). Otherwise, using the Construction Line command and trimming is a much more intuitive approach. The Construction Line and Trim commands will be covered in the next chapter.

Try it:

Draw 3 lines to form the letter 'Z'.

(Pick the Line icon)

LINE Specify first point: (Pick a point on the screen at location 1)
Specify next point or [Undo]: (Pick a point on the screen at location 2)
Specify next point or [Undo]: (Pick a point on the screen at location 3)
Specify next point or [Close/Undo]: (Pick a point on the screen at location 4)
Specify next point or [Close/Undo]: ↵

Remember, for the Line command, AutoCAD® does not know when you are done drawing lines until you exit the command by pressing the ↵ Enter key.

Circle

The Circle command creates a circle. Creating a circle and trimming it can be an easy way to create an arc. A circle can be defined in multiple ways. The default method of creating a circle using the icon is to define the center and the radius.

Procedure:

Pick (left click): **Circle icon** from the Draw Panel of the Home Tab.

The command line prompts you with the following:
CIRCLE Specify center point for circle or [3P/2P/Ttr (tan tan radius)]:

For a simple circle, pick a location for the center point:

(Pick anywhere on the screen to define the center of the circle)

After you specify the center point, the command line prompts you with the following:
Specify radius of circle or [Diameter]:

You can specify the radius of the circle by typing a value (followed by the ↵ Enter key) or by picking a second point on the screen.

If you prefer to specify the diameter instead of the radius, type the letter "**d**" (followed by the ↵ Enter key) which is for the diameter option. You do not need to click in the command line to enter the letter; simply type and the letter will be entered in the command line. After doing so, the command line will prompt you with the following:

Specify diameter of circle:

After you define the radius (or diameter, if that option was used), a circle will be created and AutoCAD® will exit the Circle command and display a command prompt.

Recommendation:

The Circle command is a very useful, easy to use tool. Circles can be used as an alternative to arcs, especially when the center point and radius are known, because a circle will become an arc after it is trimmed.

Although using circles and trimming may actually take more steps than drawing arcs using exact starting and ending points, it allows the designer not to have to think in terms of starting and ending points. After some practice, it can actually be quicker to draw this way, since less thought is involved.

Try it:

Draw a 1″ radius circle to the right of the lines you just created.

CIRCLE Specify center point for circle or [3P/2P/Ttr (tan tan radius)]: **(Pick a point on the screen at location 5)**

Specify radius of circle or [Diameter]: **1↵ (Key in the value 1 and press the ↵ Enter key)**

AutoCAD® will automatically end the Circle command.

Erase

The Erase command allows you to eliminate an object from your drawing.

Procedure:

Pick (left click): **Erase icon** from the Modify Panel of the Home Tab.

The command line prompts you with the following:

ERASE Select objects:

Select the object you want to erase by moving your cursor over the object and left-clicking the mouse to pick the object.

After you pick the first object, your command line will look like the following:

Select objects: 1 found
Select objects:

> As you pick objects to be erased, the line type changes from solid to dashed.

AutoCAD® will continue to prompt you for more objects to erase. When you are done selecting objects to erase, press the ↵ Enter key to exit the command.

Try it:

Erase the lines and circle you just created.

(Pick the Erase icon)
ERASE Select objects: **(Pick one of the lines)** *1 found*
Select objects: **(Pick another line)** *1 found, 2 total*
Select objects: **(Pick the last line)** *1 found, 3 total*
Select objects: **(Pick the circle)** *1 found, 4 total*
Select objects: ↵

> The information of how many objects found and the total is displayed above the command line.

Your screen will no longer have the lines and circle on it.

When using the Erase command, you can select objects individually or you can use either a Selection Window or a Crossing Window to select multiple objects. The following section describes the different methods of selecting objects.

Methods of Selecting Objects

Objects can be selected individually by picking them (using the left mouse button), or by using either a Selection Window or a Crossing Window. A Selection or Crossing Window allows you to select objects by picking opposite corners of a "window" around the objects you want to select. The direction in which the opposite corners are chosen determines whether you are using a Selection Window or a Crossing Window.

Selection Window (LEFT to RIGHT)

A Selection Window is used during a command and the direction of picking the opposite corners is <u>Left to Right.</u> When a Selection Window is used, only those objects that are <u>completely</u> bounded by the window are selected. If only a portion of an object is in the window, it will not be part of the selection set.

The following example of selecting one of two lines to be erased illustrates this. The area inside the Selection Window will be shaded. Only the line that is completely bounded by the window will be selected. Picking on the screen in the order shown will result in the following:

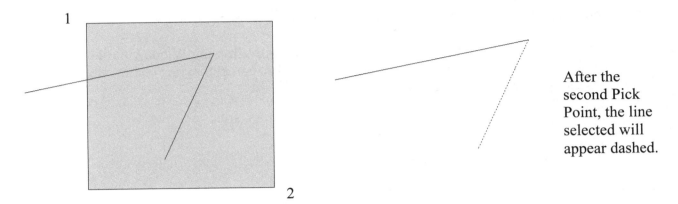

After the second Pick Point, the line selected will appear dashed.

Crossing Window (RIGHT to LEFT)

A Crossing Window is used during a command and the direction of picking the opposite corners is Right to Left. When a Crossing Window is used, objects that are bounded by the window are selected, including those that only a portion of which crosses the window.

The following example of selecting two lines to be erased illustrates this. The area inside the Crossing Window will be shaded. Although only a portion of one line is completely bounded by the window, a portion of it will be selected. Picking on the screen in the order shown will result in the following:

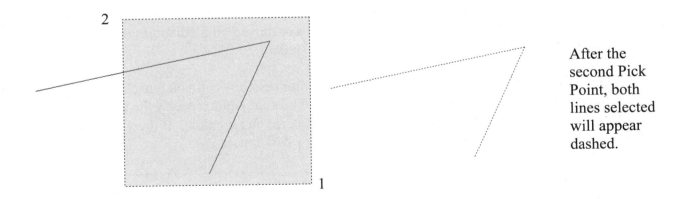

After the second Pick Point, both lines selected will appear dashed.

Notice that the Selection Window boundary is shown as a solid line and a Crossing Window boundary is shown as a dashed line. In addition, the color of the area inside the Crossing Window is different from the color of the Selection Window.

Removing Objects from the Selection Set

When selecting multiple objects, you may have selected more objects than was intended. To remove objects from the selection set, simply hold the shift key and select the objects to remove. The selection method is the same: individual, selection window, or crossing window.

Using the same example as above (both lines were selected with Crossing Window during the Erase command), we can remove one of the two lines selected before completing the command. The following is the command line sequence:

ERASE Select objects:

Use a Crossing Window to select both lines

Specify opposite corner: 2 found

Once the 2 lines are selected, hold the shift key and pick the line you want to remove from the selection set.

Select objects: 1 found, 1 removed, 1 total

Select objects: ⏎

Pressing the ⏎ Enter key completes the Erase command.

Grips

Sometime while trying out AutoCAD®, you may occasionally notice that your objects are highlighted and have little blue boxes attached to them. Or you may have moved your cursor on the screen and found that AutoCAD® appears to be drawing a rectangle (it isn't).

This can occur when you do not have a command in the command line and you left-click somewhere on your screen. After you do this, your command line will prompt you to specify the opposite corner. AutoCAD® is attempting to create a selection window or a crossing window. If there are objects selected without a command in the command line, the grips will appear.

Picking objects without having an active command will place grips on them.

Grips can be used to change object locations and sizes. For example, a line will have three grips attached to it: one at each end, and one at the mid-point. Picking the grip at the midpoint will allow you to relocate the line on your screen. Picking either end grip will allow you to change the length and angle of the line – this occurs because you are moving only one endpoint while the other endpoint stays fixed.

If you have no intention of using grips and you accidentally get them on your screen, simply press the Escape (Esc) key to make them go away.

> Pressing the Esc key will remove the grips from your objects.

Zoom and Pan

The Zoom and Pan features within AutoCAD® allow you to view the drawing you are creating at different sizes and locations. Imagine that the drawing you are creating is similar to the paper on a drawing board and you are viewing your drawing through a camera lens. The Zoom feature allows you to get a close-up look at an area or get a wider view, depending on whether you zoom in on a specific area or zoom out. The Pan feature moves the camera side-to-side or top-to-bottom.

There are several methods to Zoom and Pan around your drawing. One of the easiest methods of zooming in and out and panning is to use the wheel on the wheel mouse.

Zoom and Pan Using the Wheel Mouse

Wheel

Wheel Mouse

Rolling the wheel forward and aft allows you to zoom in and out of the drawing. Pressing the wheel down will change the cursor from a pointer to a hand. Moving the mouse around, while pressing the wheel down, allows you to "pan" around your drawing. This feature can come in handy because you do not need to select an icon or key in a command. In addition, you can zoom and pan using the wheel while you are in the middle of a command.

You can also fill your drawing screen with all the objects you have drawn by double-clicking the wheel on the mouse. This is referred to as Zoom Extents.

Typing the Zoom Command

One method of zooming is to type the command. Typing the letter "z" is the shortcut for the zoom command.

> _ z ↵

> Because the prompt is lengthy, some of it appears above the active section of the command line.

ZOOM
Specify corner of window, enter a scale factor (nX or nXP), or
ZOOM [All/Center/Dynamic/Extents/Previous/Scale/Window/Object] <real time>:

AutoCAD® will default to a Zoom Window command. A Zoom Window allows you to pick opposite corners of a selected area on your drawing to enlarge that area to fill your screen.

You can choose one of the multiple options shown in the square brackets. For instance, if you wanted to zoom the entire drawing, type the letter "a" for All. Each option is the same as previously explained.

Example of Zoom Window:

If you had the following items on your screen and you want to zoom in on just the circles, select the Zoom command by typing the letter "z" and then pressing the ↵ Enter key. This will begin the Zoom command. Now simply pick opposite corners around the circles (shown here at locations 1 and 2):

As you move your cursor from location 1 to location 2, you will notice what looks like a rectangle growing on the screen as it follows your cursor. That is the Zoom Window. You must left-click point 2 to complete the Zoom Window. After the second point is selected, the command will end. Only those items in that window will now fill the screen. Depending on the shape of the Zoom Window, some additional pieces of other items may also appear on your screen.

Recommendation:

I have found that using the wheel mouse is the easiest way to zoom and pan around the drawing. In addition, double-clicking the wheel mouse is the easiest way to see the extent of everything you have drawn.

Summary

In this chapter you have learned to:

- Change the units from decimal to feet and inches.
- Create lines and circles
- Erase objects
- Select objects or remove objects from a selection set
- Get grips and make them disappear
- Navigate through your drawing using the Zoom command and mouse wheel

Review Questions

1. How do you change the units from decimal to feet and inches?

2. How does the line command end?

3. How does the circle command end?

4. When you erase objects, how do you know they were selected?

5. What is the difference between a crossing window and a selection window?

6. What are the blue boxes called and how did they get there?

7. How do you get rid of the blue boxes if you get them?

8. How do you use the wheel on your mouse to move around the drawing?

9. What is the shortcut key for the Zoom command?

10. What is a Zoom Window?

Exercises

1. Draw the star. Do not concern yourself with size or location.

2. Draw the patch. Do not concern yourself with size or location.

3. Draw the circles. Do not concern yourself with size or location.

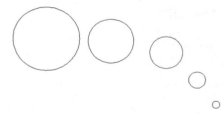

4. Draw the lines and circle. Do not concern yourself with size or location.

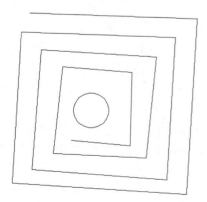

Chapter 3
Commands – Set 1: Drawing Construction – Getting Started

Learning Objectives:

- A familiar shape: Rectangle
- Change rectangles to lines by using Explode
- Creating parallel or concentric objects using Offset
- Creating Horizontal, Vertical, Angled, and Offset Construction Lines
- Changing the object limits using Trim, Extend, and Lengthen
- Improving drawing accuracy using Object Snap

In Chapter 2 we learned two basic drawing commands and one modify command to help us get started drawing: Line, Circle, and Erase. Not enough information was given in that chapter to allow you to create a drawing with accuracy. In this chapter we will learn more commands that will help us create an accurate drawing. We will also learn AutoCAD® construction techniques that will help you to make drawings quickly.

We will start with a shape that is most familiar to us: the rectangle. From there, we will move on to creating infinitely long lines, known as construction lines. The nice part about construction lines is that you can make them horizontal, vertical or at a specific angle. This can also be done with the Line command, however, I have found that the construction lines are much easier to work with.

Of course, infinitely long lines are not what we want as the final product. We will learn how to trim those lines. In addition, if a line is too short, we will learn how to extend it.

And finally, there are times when we need to connect a line or a circle to an endpoint, or maybe draw a line through a center of the circle. Using the Object Snap feature of AutoCAD® will allow us to create drawings with complete accuracy.

Rectangle

The Rectangle command has several options: Chamfer, Elevation, Fillet, Thickness, and Width, as well as a prompt for the corners of the rectangle. These options allow you to manipulate the appearance and the placement of the rectangle before it is drawn. Chamfer and Fillet are options that change the corners of the rectangle. We will not be using the other options.

Procedure:

Pick (left click): **Rectangle icon** from the Draw Panel of the Home Tab.

The command line prompts you with the following:

RECTANG *Specify first corner point or [Chamfer/Elevation/Fillet/Thickness/Width]:*

For a simple rectangle, anchor the first corner by picking anywhere on the screen or by picking a point on an existing object (must have OSNAP turned on or select an object snap override before picking – more about this later).

After you specify the first corner point, the command line prompts you with the following:

Specify other corner point or [Area/Dimensions/Rotation]:

You can specify the second corner by simply picking a second point on the screen. Of course, this will not let you know the size of the rectangle that was created.

A recommended method to create a rectangle of a specific size is to type "d" for *Dimensions* and then press the ⏎ Enter key. In the command line, AutoCAD® will prompt you for the size of the rectangle in two steps. The first prompt is for the horizontal direction. The second prompt is for the vertical direction. Unfortunately, the wording of the prompts is confusing.

> *Length* is the AutoCAD® prompt word for horizontal direction.
> *Width* is the AutoCAD® prompt word for vertical direction.

AutoCAD® prompts for the horizontal direction as follows:

Specify length for rectangles <X'-X''>:   Note: *X'-X''* represents any number
At this prompt type in the distance for the rectangle in the horizontal direction and press the ⏎ Enter key.

AutoCAD® prompts for the vertical direction as follows:

Specify width for rectangles <Y'-Y''>:   Note: *Y'-Y''* represents any number
At this prompt type in the distance for the rectangle in the vertical direction and press the ⏎ Enter key.

AutoCAD® has one more prompt. Because we have specified the location of one corner and the size of the rectangle, there still remain 4 choices for the opposite corner. The prompt is as follows:

Specify other corner point or [Area/Dimensions/Rotation]:

Using your cursor, pick the location of the second corner of the rectangle. Note that there are four locations that can be picked (upper right, upper left, lower left, lower right). As you move your cursor around, the rectangle will follow for each location.

After you pick the second corner point, the Rectangle command is complete and you are back to the command prompt.

The rectangle is considered to be a single object, and as such can be erased completely by picking anywhere on the rectangle.

Recommendation:

Use rectangles for the start of the room walls, drawing format borders, furniture or other rectangular shaped objects. The advantage of using rectangles is that they can be offset by using a single Offset command (more info on Offset appears later in this chapter). All four sides will be offset and trimmed at once. This is a time saver for walls. For ease of drawing, use the dimension option for the second corner. Doing it this way allows the designer not to have to think in X-Y coordinates.

If you use rectangles, it is recommended that you then convert them to lines (after you are done offsetting them). This is done by using the Explode command. Lines are then treated as individual objects and are easier to modify.

Try it:

Draw an 8′ x 16′ rectangle. Make sure you have Units set to Architectural before you start.

(Pick the Rectangle icon)
RECTANG Specify first corner point or [Chamfer/Elevation/Fillet/Thickness/Width]:
(Pick a point on the screen at location 1)

Specify other corner point or [Area/Dimensions/Rotation]: **d↵**
(Key in the letter "d" and press the ↵ Enter key)

Although it is prompting for length, AutoCAD® is looking for the value for the horizontal direction:
Specify length for rectangles <8'-0">: **16′↵ (Key in 16′ and press the ↵ Enter key)**

Although it is prompting for width, AutoCAD® is looking for the value for the vertical direction
Specify width for rectangles <16'-0">: **8′↵ (Key in 8′ and press the ↵ Enter key)**

Specify other corner point or [Area/Dimensions/Rotation]: (Pick a point on the screen at location 2)

AutoCAD® ends the command and your rectangle is on the screen.

Explode

The Explode command allows you to break down a compound object to its basic components. As an example, a rectangle is made up of 4 lines. However, AutoCAD® treats a rectangle as a single object. If you explode a rectangle, it will still appear as a rectangle on your screen, but AutoCAD® now treats it as 4 separate lines.

Procedure:

Pick (left click): **Explode icon** from the Modify Panel of the Home Tab.

Explode icon

The command line prompts you with the following:

EXPLODE Select objects:

Select the object to explode by moving your cursor over the object and left-clicking the mouse to pick the object.

After you pick the first object, your command lines will look like the following:

Select objects: 1 found
Select objects:

AutoCAD® will continue to prompt you for more objects to explode. When you are done selecting objects to Explode, press the ↵ Enter key to exit the command.

Recommendation:

Typically used for converting rectangles to lines. If you use rectangles, it is recommended that you then convert them to lines (after you are done offsetting them). This is done by using the Explode command. Lines are then treated as individual objects and are easier to modify.

Explode is also useful for converting Blocks to individual objects. Blocks will be covered in a later chapter.

Try it:

Hold your cursor over the rectangle that you just created. The rectangle will be highlighted and become bold lines and a tip will pop up identifying this object as a Polyline. A Polyline is what AutoCAD® names the rectangle.

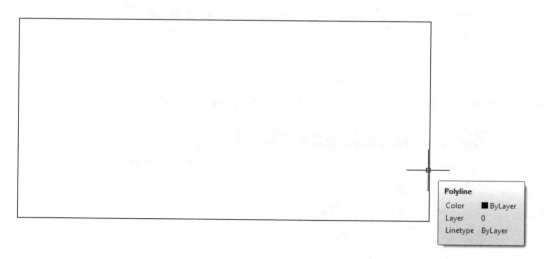

Now let's break down the rectangle into 4 separate lines by using the Explode command.

(Pick the Explode icon)

EXPLODE *Select objects:* **(Pick the rectangle)** *1 found*
Select objects: ⏎
Pressing the ⏎ Enter key exits the command and the command prompt returns.

Now hold your cursor over any of the lines of the rectangle and your pop up tip will tell you that it found a line. The line will be highlighted, not the whole rectangle.

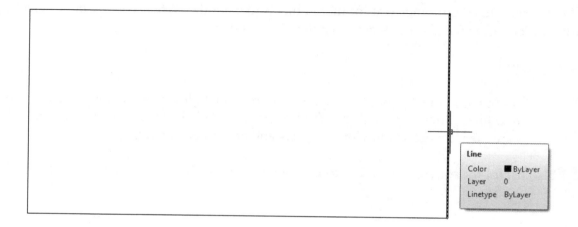

Offset

The Offset command creates parallel lines or curves, and concentric circles or rectangles/polygons, a specified distance away or through a specified point. This is used to create new objects from existing ones.

Procedure:

Pick (left click): **Offset icon** from the Modify Panel of the Home Tab.

Offset icon

The command line prompts you with the following:

***OFFSET** Specify offset distance or [Through/Erase/Layer] <X'-XX">:*

Key in a specified distance you wish to offset, followed by pressing the ⏎ Enter key.
You can also accept the default of *<X'-XX">* by pressing the ⏎ Enter key.

Note that the value inside the brackets is the value that was previously used in an Offset command. If this is the first time the Offset command is used for the drawing, the value would be *Through*.

After specifying the distance, the command line prompts you with the following:

Select object to offset or [Exit/Undo] <Exit>:
Select the object by left-clicking the mouse when the cursor is over the object you wish to select.

After selecting the object you wish to offset, the command line prompts you with the following:

Specify point of side to offset or [Exit/Multiple/Undo] <Exit>:

For specifying the point of side to offset, there are two choices that can be made here. As an example, a vertical line can be offset to the left or to the right. A circle, rectangle, or polygon, can be offset inside or outside. To specify which side to offset, left-click the mouse when the cursor is on the side of the object you wish to offset.

AutoCAD® will continue to prompt for more objects to offset:
Select object to offset or [Exit/Undo] <Exit>:

To exit the command, press the ⏎ Enter key.

Recommendation:

The Offset command is a very useful tool, and likely the most used command. If you have lines on the drawing to offset, but they are not as long as you would like them to be after they are offset, then it is more convenient to use the Construction Line command (next topic) with the Offset option. An example would be if you had the interior walls drawn and want to construct the exterior walls. Using Offset would leave a gap at the corners. Trimming/Extending cannot be used. You can use Fillet with a Radius=0 (Fillet command will be covered in the next chapter) to close them, however, it is easier to avoid this situation by using a Construction Line Offset instead.

Try it:

Anywhere on your screen, draw a line, a circle, and a rectangle. All objects are an arbitrary size, but should at least be about 12″ in size. We will then offset each of these objects by 2″.

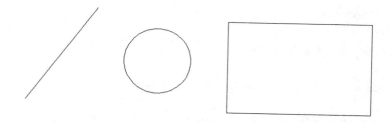

(Pick the Offset icon)

OFFSET *Current settings: Erase source=No Layer=Source OFFSETGAPTYPE=0*
Specify offset distance or [Through/Erase/Layer] <Through>: **2↵**
(Type "2" and press the ↵ Enter key)

Select object to offset or [Exit/Undo] <Exit>: **(Pick the line)**
Specify point on side to offset or [Exit/Multiple/Undo] <Exit>: **(Pick to the right of the line)**

Select object to offset or [Exit/Undo] <Exit>: **(Pick the circle)**
Specify point on side to offset or [Exit/Multiple/Undo] <Exit>: **(Pick outside the circle)**

Select object to offset or [Exit/Undo] <Exit>: **(Pick the rectangle)**
Specify point on side to offset or [Exit/Multiple/Undo] <Exit>: **(Pick outside the rectangle)**

Select object to offset or [Exit/Undo] <Exit>: ↵ **(Press the ↵ Enter key to exit the command)**

When you are done, your drawing will look like this:

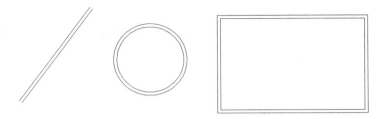

<u>Construction Line</u>

The Construction Line command creates a line (through a point that you select) that extends infinitely in both directions from the first point selected. You can select options at the command prompt to draw a horizontal, vertical, or angled construction line, or to offset the construction line by a distance from the object that you specify.

<u>Procedure:</u>

Pick (left click): Pick the pull-down arrow to expand the Draw Panel of the Home Tab. Pick the **Construction Line icon**.

Construction Line icon

Push-Pin

Because the Construction Line icon is not displayed in the first row, the Draw Panel needs to be expanded by using the down arrow. The Draw Panel can remain expanded if you desire by selecting the Push-Pin. When selected, its appearance will change:

To unpin it, pick it again.

The command line prompts you with the following:
XLINE Specify a point or [Hor/Ver/Ang/Bisect/Offset]:

For a simple construction line, anchor the first point by either picking anywhere on the screen (with or without grid/snap turned on), or picking a point on existing object (must have OSNAP turned on or select an object snap override, which is covered later, before picking).

After you specify the first point, the command line prompts you with the following:
Specify through point:

You can specify the second point, or "through point" by picking anywhere on the screen or picking a specific point on an existing object.

After you select the "through point", the construction line will be created and another one will follow your cursor, coming from the same first point. AutoCAD® will continue prompting for more "through points":
Specify through point:

When you are finished with putting construction lines on your drawing, press the ↵ Enter key to exit the Construction Line command.

Construction Line Options

Horizontal and Vertical Construction Lines

For a horizontal or vertical construction line, type the letter "v" or "h" at the Construction Line prompt and then press the ↵ Enter key.

Note that the construction line will appear on your screen and will follow your cursor and prompt you as follows:
Specify through point:

The methods of specifying the "through point" are the same as previously described.

After you select the "through point", the construction line will be created and another one will follow your cursor. AutoCAD® will continue prompting for more "through points":

When you are finished with putting construction lines on your drawing, press the ↵ Enter key to exit the Construction Line command.

Angled Construction Lines

For an angled construction line, type the letter "a" at the construction line prompt and then press the ↵ Enter key. The command line prompts you with the following:

Enter angle of xline (0) or [Reference]:

Type in the desired angle of the construction line and then press the ↵ Enter key. The command line prompts you with the following:
Specify through point:

From here on, the command acts the same as the horizontal or vertical line options.

Offset Option

This option works the same as the Offset command, only it puts construction lines in. You must key in the distance and select the direction to offset.

Recommendation:

The Construction Line command is a very useful tool. Horizontal, vertical, and angled lines are the most commonly used options. The Offset option can also be very useful. The Bisect option is rarely used and is not described here. It is left to the student to explore this option if so desired.

After construction lines are put on the drawing, it is necessary to trim them using the Trim command (discussed in the next section).

Although using construction lines and trimming may actually take more steps than drawing lines exactly where you want them by using X-Y coordinates, it allows the designer not to have to think in terms of X-Y coordinates. After some practice, it can actually be quicker to draw this way, since less thought is involved.

Try it:

1. **Draw 5 horizontal lines anywhere on your screen.**

(Pick the Construction Line icon)

XLINE *Specify a point or [Hor/Ver/Ang/Bisect/Offset]:* **h↵**
(Type "h" and press the ↵ Enter key)

Specify through point: (Pick a location anywhere on your screen)
Specify through point: (Pick a location anywhere on your screen)
Specify through point: (Pick a location anywhere on your screen)
Specify through point: (Pick a location anywhere on your screen)
Specify through point: (Pick a location anywhere on your screen)
Specify through point: ↵ **(Press the ↵ Enter key to exit the command)**

2. Draw 5 vertical lines anywhere on your screen.

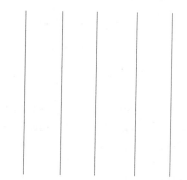

(Pick the Construction Line icon)

XLINE Specify a point or [Hor/Ver/Ang/Bisect/Offset]: **v↵**
(Type "v" and press the ↵ Enter key)

Specify through point: **(Pick a location anywhere on your screen)**
Specify through point: **(Pick a location anywhere on your screen)**
Specify through point: **(Pick a location anywhere on your screen)**
Specify through point: **(Pick a location anywhere on your screen)**
Specify through point: **(Pick a location anywhere on your screen)**
Specify through point: ↵ **(Press the ↵ Enter key to exit the command)**

3. Draw a 45° angled line anywhere on your screen.

(Pick the Construction Line icon)

XLINE Specify a point or [Hor/Ver/Ang/Bisect/Offset]: **a↵**
(Type "a" and press the ↵ Enter key)

Enter angle of xline (0) or [Reference]: **45↵**
(Type "45" and press the ↵ Enter key)

Specify through point: **(Pick a location on the screen for your line)**
Specify through point: ↵ **(Press the ↵ Enter key to exit the command)**

4. Draw a 4″ Construction Line offset.

Draw a line anywhere on your screen. The length and angle is arbitrary.

Now we will create an infinitely long line parallel to this one.
(Pick the Construction Line icon)

XLINE Specify a point or [Hor/Ver/Ang/Bisect/Offset]: **o↵**
(Type "o" and press the ↵ Enter key)
Specify offset distance or [Through] <0'-2">: **4↵**
(Type "4" and press the ↵ Enter key)

Select a line object: ***(Pick the line)***
Specify side to offset: ***(Pick to the right of the line)***
Select a line object: **↵ (Press the ↵ Enter key to exit the command)**

When you are done, your drawing will look like this:

Changing Object Limits

The Trim command and the Extend command allow you to change the limits of existing objects. Trimming will shorten or cut out a section of an object. Extending will allow you to increase the length of an object (within the limits of the objects definition). One command can be used to perform the same as the other by holding the shift key during the object selection process. Both commands require specific cutting or boundary edges to define the endpoint location.

Lengthen allows you to drag an endpoint of a line or arc to lengthen or shorten it, without requiring you to define a specific cutting edge or boundary edge.

Trim

Trim is a two-part command; the first part is to select cutting edges, and the second part is to select the objects to trim to those cutting edges. In order to trim an object, AutoCAD® requires the designer to first identify a "cutting edge". You can think of a cutting edge as a knife that will slice through the object you plan to trim. The cutting edge does not have to pass through the object you plan to trim; it can also project through the object (as long as *Edge=Extend* is set). The Trim command can also perform as an Extend command by holding the shift key down while picking the object to extend (it will treat the cutting edge as a boundary edge instead).

Procedure:

Pick (left click): **Trim icon** from the Modify Panel of the Home Tab.

Trim
icon

The command line prompts you with the following:

Current settings: Projection=UCS, Edge=None
Select cutting edges ...
***TRIM** Select objects or <select all>:*

> Information related to the command will appear above the command line. It is represented in the book as shadowed text.

There can be more than one cutting edge. These can be selected by the following methods:

1.   Individually
2.   Using a Selection Window or Crossing Window
3.   Pressing the ↵ Enter key to select all objects as cutting edges

When an object is found as a cutting edge, AutoCAD® will highlight that object by changing its appearance to a dashed line. If it is already a dashed line, the size of the dashes becomes smaller. The exception to this is when the ↵ Enter key is used to select all objects as cutting edges.

Since AutoCAD® does not know in advance how many cutting edges the designer wishes to select, it will continue to prompt with the following:

Select objects: 1 found
Select objects:

After selecting all the cutting edges desired, press the ↵ Enter key. This will bring you to the second part of the command, which will prompt you with the following:

Select object to trim or shift-select to extend or
[Fence/Crossing/Project/Edge/eRase/Undo]:

You now have several options:

1. Pick the object to trim, or
2. Hold down the shift key and select an object to extend (the cutting edge will now act as a boundary edge), or
3. Choose one of the options in the [ ] brackets by typing the letter of the option that is capitalized.

Option 1

To select the object to trim, move the cursor to the object you wish to trim, on the portion of the object you want to eliminate, and use the left mouse button to pick that object.

Example:

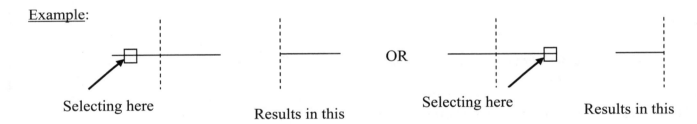

Selecting here   Results in this   OR   Selecting here   Results in this

You can also select a portion of an object to trim that is between two cutting edges:

Example:

Selecting here   Results in this

Option 2

This option works the same as the Extend command. Refer to the instructions for that command.

Option 3

We will describe only one of the choices in the square brackets: [*Undo*]

Use this choice if an object was trimmed in error. This must be done after an object was trimmed and while you are still in the command. Simply type the letter "u" followed by the ↵ Enter key.

Select object to trim or shift-select to extend or
[Fence/Crossing/Project/Edge/eRase/Undo]: **u** ↵

Try it:

Draw any size rectangle anywhere on your screen. Draw a horizontal construction line passing through the rectangle.

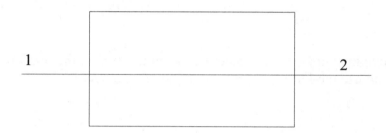

Now we will use the Trim command to trim the construction line to the rectangle.
(Pick the Trim icon)
`
Current settings: Projection=UCS, Edge=None
Select cutting edges ...
TRIM *Select objects or <select all>:* **(Pick the Rectangle)** *1 found*
Select objects: ↵ **(Press the ↵ Enter key to get to the second part of the command)**

Select object to trim or shift-select to extend or
[Fence/Crossing/Project/Edge/eRase/Undo]: **(Pick the Construction Line near point 1)**

Select object to trim or shift-select to extend or
[Fence/Crossing/Project/Edge/eRase/Undo]: **(Pick the Construction Line near point 2)**

Select object to trim or shift-select to extend or
[Fence/Crossing/Project/Edge/eRase/Undo]: ↵ **(Press the ↵ Enter key to exit the command)**

When you are done, your drawing will look like this:

Try it:

Let's try this again, only our new goal is to remove the portion of the construction line that passes through the rectangle.

Draw any size rectangle anywhere on your screen. Draw a horizontal construction line passing through the rectangle.

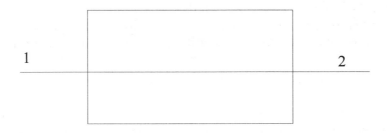

Now we will use the Trim command to trim the construction line to the rectangle.

(Pick the Trim icon)

Current settings: Projection=UCS, Edge=None
Select cutting edges ...
TRIM Select objects or <select all>: *(Pick the Rectangle)* *1 found*
Select objects: ↵ **(Press the ↵ Enter key to get to the second part of the command)**

Select object to trim or shift-select to extend or
[Fence/Crossing/Project/Edge/eRase/Undo]: *(Pick the Construction Line inside the rectangle)*

Select object to trim or shift-select to extend or
[Fence/Crossing/Project/Edge/eRase/Undo]: ↵ **(Press the ↵ Enter key to exit the command)**

When you are done, your drawing will look like this:

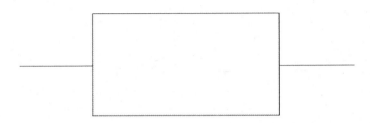

Extend

Extend is a two-part command; the first part is to select boundary edges, and the second part is to select the objects to extend to those boundary edges. In order to extend an object, AutoCAD® requires the designer to first identify a "boundary edge". You can think of a boundary edge as a wall that will stop the object from extending beyond. The boundary edge does not have to be in the path of the object you plan to extend; it can also project through the path of the object (as long as *Edge=Extend* is set). The Extend command can also perform as a Trim command by holding the shift key down while picking the object to trim (it will treat the boundary edge as a cutting edge instead).

Procedure:

Pick (left click): Pick the pull-down arrow next to the Trim Command in the Modify Panel of the Home Tab. Pick the **Extend icon**.

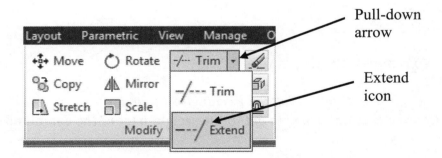

The command line prompts you with the following:

Current settings: Projection=UCS, Edge=None
Select boundary edges ...
EXTEND *Select objects or <select all>:*

There can be more than one boundary edge. These can be selected by the following methods:

1. Individually
2. Using a Selection Window or Crossing Window
3. Pressing the ↵ Enter key to select all objects as boundary edges

When an object is found as a boundary edge, AutoCAD® will highlight that object by changing its appearance to a dashed line. If it is already a dashed line, the size of the dashes becomes smaller. The exception to this is when the ↵ Enter key is used to select all objects as boundary edges.

Since AutoCAD® does not know in advance how many boundary edges the designer wishes to select, it will continue to prompt with the following:

Select objects: 1 found
Select objects:

After selecting all the boundary edges desired, press the ↵ Enter key. This will bring you to the second part of the command, which will prompt you with the following:

Select object to extend or shift-select to trim or
[Fence/Crossing/Project/Edge/Undo]:

You now have several options:

1. Pick the object to extend, or
2. Hold down the shift key and select an object to trim (the boundary edge will now act as a cutting edge), or
3. Choose one of the options in the [ ] brackets by typing the letter of the option that is capitalized.

<u>Option 1</u>

To select the object to extend, move the cursor to the object you wish to extend, on the portion of the object you want to increase in length, and use the left mouse button to pick that object.

<u>Example:</u>

Selecting here   Results in this

Option 2

This option works the same as the Trim command. Refer to the instructions for that command.

Option 3

We will describe only one of the choices in the square brackets: [*Undo*]
Use this choice if an object was extended in error. This must be done after an object was extended and while you are still in the command. Simply type the letter "u" followed by the ↵ Enter key.

Select object to extend or shift-select to trim or
[Fence/Crossing/Project/Edge/Undo]: **u** ↵

Try it:

Draw two lines on your screen like these:

Now extend Line "A" to Line "B"

(Pick the Extend icon)

Current settings: Projection=UCS, Edge=None
Select boundary edges ...
EXTEND *Select objects or <select all>:* **(Pick Line "B")** *1 found*

Select objects: ↵ **(Pressing the ↵ Enter key will get you to the second part of the command)**

Select object to extend or shift-select to trim or
[Fence/Crossing/Project/Edge/Undo]: **(Pick Line "A" near the endpoint marked 1)**

Select object to extend or shift-select to trim or
[Fence/Crossing/Project/Edge/Undo]: ↵ **(Pressing the ↵ Enter key will end the command)**

When you are done, your drawing will look like this:

Lengthen

Lengthen can be used as an alternative to Trim and Extend. There are several options available for the Lengthen command, but only the Dynamic option will be covered. This option supplements the Trim and Extend commands (rather than be an alternative). It allows you to drag an endpoint of a line or arc to lengthen or shorten it, without requiring you to define a specific cutting edge or boundary edge.

Procedure:

Pick (left click): Pick the pull-down arrow to expand the Modify Panel of the Home Tab. Pick the **Lengthen icon**.

The command line prompts you with the following:

LENGTHEN Select an object or [DElta/Percent/Total/DYnamic]: **dy⏎**
(Type "dy" and press the ⏎ Enter key)

Select an object to change or [Undo]
(Pick either a line or an arc near the endpoint you want changed)

Specify new end point:
(Pick a location on the drawing space to define the location of the new endpoint)

AutoCAD® will continue to prompt for more objects to change:
Select an object to change or [Undo]:

To exit the command, press the ⏎ Enter key.

Try it:

Draw three lines anywhere on your screen.

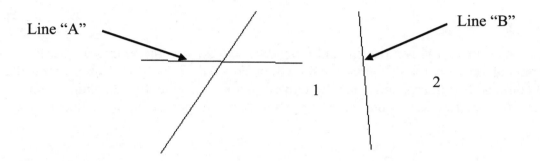

Line "A"   Line "B"

1   2

Now we will use the Lengthen command to extend line A beyond line B.

(Pick the Lengthen icon)

LENGTHEN Select an object or [DElta/Percent/Total/DYnamic]: **dy⏎**
Select an object to change or [Undo]: **(Pick Line "A" near the endpoint marked 1)**
Specify new end point: **(Pick near location 2)**
Select an object to change or [Undo]: ⏎ **(Pressing the ⏎ Enter key will end the command)**

When you are done, your drawing will look like this:

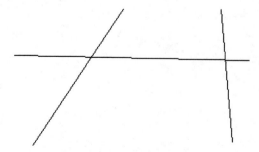

This command works the same way with arcs. Later in the book you will learn about arcs. Once you have an arc on your screen, you can try this command again.

Object Snap – OSNAP

A major advantage of using AutoCAD®, or most Computer Aided Design programs, is the precision in which you can draw. To place objects in a precise location, such as the end of a line, the center of a circle, etc., AutoCAD® provides two methods: OSNAP and Object Snap. OSNAP is an abbreviation for Object Snap. When it is turned on, it can be thought of as a Running OSNAP.

OSNAP icon

On the lower part of your screen, you will see the following: Object Snap icon

The Object Snap icon is a button that can be turned on and off. Move your cursor over the Object Snap icon and left-click to turn on the OSNAP feature. When OSNAP is turned on, the button will appear shaded blue.

There are many settings within OSNAP that can be turned on. To change those settings, hold your cursor over the OSNAP button and right-click. A pop-up box will appear by your cursor:

Each choice has an icon to the left of it. If the icon has a square box around it, that choice is selected. In this example, Endpoint, Midpoint, Center, and Intersection are selected. To select or de-select, pick on the icon. These are done one at a time. However, this method can be a little confusing and you may unintentionally turn the OSNAP feature off.

A surer method of selecting which Object Snap choices you want is to pick Settings…
A Drafting Settings dialog box will appear. You can individually select your choice by picking the check box so that a check mark appears. Pick the OK button to exit the dialog box.

Using the OSNAP feature

Example 1. - Endpoint

In this example, let's place the center of a circle at the lowest end of the right vertical line of the three lines shown:

Notice that as the cursor gets near the endpoint of the line, an AutoSnap marker will appear at the end of the line, and a "tip" will indicate "Endpoint". Once the AutoSnap marker appears, left-click to pick the end of the line.

Pick anywhere away from that endpoint to complete the circle.

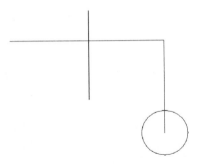

Example 2. – Intersection

Now let's place the center of a circle at the intersection of the left vertical line and the horizontal line:

Notice that as the cursor gets near the intersection of the two lines, an AutoSnap marker will appear at the intersection, and a "tip" will indicate "Intersection". Once the AutoSnap marker appears, left-click to pick the intersection.

Pick anywhere away from that endpoint to complete the circle.

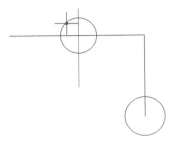

Object Snaps – Override

Object Snaps work very similar to OSNAP, except that these are one-time use overrides. Use Object Snaps when you are in the middle of a particular command to make your selection snap to a particular portion of an object. This can be done with OSNAP turned off or on. If OSNAP is turned on, you can override the OSNAP selection by selecting a particular Object Snap command from the Object Snap toolbar.

The Object Snap toolbar is not on the ribbon. However, it can be turned on by the User Interface panel of the View tab. Select the pull-down arrow of the Toolbars icon and then select AutoCAD from the choices presented. A list of available toolbars will appear.

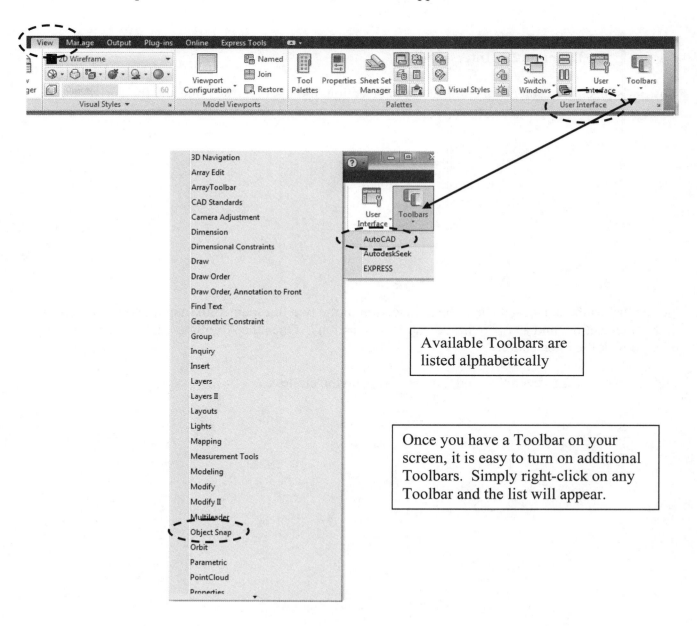

Available Toolbars are listed alphabetically

Once you have a Toolbar on your screen, it is easy to turn on additional Toolbars. Simply right-click on any Toolbar and the list will appear.

Once you select Object Snap from the list of Toolbar choices, the Object Snap toolbar will appear "floating" on your drawing space. You can dock your toolbar as described in Chapter 1.

Object Snap Toolbar

Example 3.

Let's add another circle to the horizontal line, but we need to add it to the midpoint of the line. Note that the midpoint of the line is very close to the intersection of the lines where the circle was created in example 2. If we leave OSNAP turned on, AutoCAD® will try to find the intersection of the two lines as the cursor gets near the intersection. We can override this by selecting the Snap to Midpoint icon from the Object Snap toolbar while we are in the middle of the *Circle* command.

CIRCLE Specify center point for circle or [3P/2P/Ttr (tan tan radius)]: **(Pick Snap to Midpoint icon)**

CIRCLE Specify center point for circle or [3P/2P/Ttr (tan tan radius)]: _mid of **(Pick the midpoint of the horizontal line)**

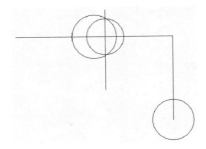

Notice that as the cursor gets near the midpoint of the line, an AutoSnap marker will appear at the intersection, and a "tip" will indicate "Midpoint". Once the AutoSnap marker appears, left-click to pick the midpoint.

Pick anywhere away from the midpoint to complete the circle.

Try it:

Locate the circle inside the rectangle by using Construction Line Offset:

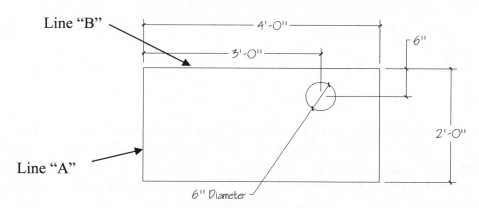

Before beginning, make sure that Object Snap icon on your Status Bar is turned on and that Intersection is selected. Ignore the default values shown.

(Pick the Rectangle icon)

RECTANG Specify first corner point or [Chamfer/Elevation/Fillet/Thickness/Width]:
Specify other corner point or [Area/Dimensions/Rotation]: **d⏎**
Specify length for rectangles <16'-0">: **4'⏎**
Specify width for rectangles <8'-0">: **2'⏎**
Specify other corner point or [Area/Dimensions/Rotation]: **(Pick for the opposite corner location)**

(Pick the Construction Line icon)

XLINE Specify a point or [Hor/Ver/Ang/Bisect/Offset]: **o⏎**
Specify offset distance or [Through] <0'-4">: **3'⏎**
Select a line object: **(Pick the rectangle line "A")**
Specify side to offset: **(Pick to the right of the selected line)**
Select a line object: ⏎

Press the ⏎ Enter key to repeat the Construction Line command

XLINE Specify a point or [Hor/Ver/Ang/Bisect/Offset]: **o⏎**
Specify offset distance or [Through] <3'-0">: **6⏎**
Select a line object: **(Pick the rectangle line "B")**
Specify side to offset: **(Pick below the selected line)**
Select a line object: ⏎

We now have intersecting construction lines that define the center of the circle. With OSNAP turned on and set to look for Intersections, we can proceed to put the circle in the exact location.

(Pick the Circle icon)

CIRCLE Specify center point for circle or [3P/2P/Ttr (tan tan radius)]:
(Pick the Intersection of the Construction Lines)

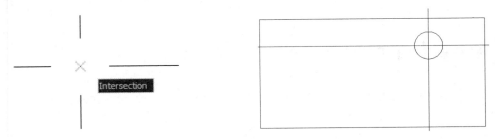

Specify radius of circle or [Diameter] <0'-3">: **d⏎**
Specify diameter of circle <0'-6">: **6⏎**

The circle is now drawn exactly 6″ diameter exactly located in the rectangle. All we need to do now is to eliminate the construction lines to complete the drawing. Use the Erase command to do this.

(Pick Erase icon)

ERASE Select objects: (Pick the vertical construction line) 1 found
Select objects: (Pick the horizontal construction line) 1 found, 2 total
Select objects: ⏎

When you are done, your drawing will look like this:

Summary

In this chapter you have learned to:

- Create rectangles of specific size
- Change the rectangle object to individual lines using Explode
- Create parallel lines and concentric rectangles or circles using Offset
- Create infinitely long lines that are horizontal, vertical, or at a specific angle
- Create an infinitely long line parallel to an existing line object using the Offset option of the Construction line command
- Change the length of lines using either Trim, Extend, or Lengthen
- Place your objects at precise locations using the OSNAP or Object Snap tools

Review Questions

1. What is the option in the Rectangle command that allows you to create a rectangle of a specific size?

2. After you type in the size of the rectangle, what is the final step needed to complete the Rectangle command?

3. What command do you use to convert a rectangle into 4 separate lines?

4. What command is used to create a line parallel to another line?

5. How do you create an infinitely long parallel line?

6. How many steps are involved with creating an Offset?

7. How do you create horizontal, vertical, or angled lines that are infinitely long?

8. To change the length of a line, which two commands can be used?

9. Which icon on the Status Bar must be turned on to draw accurately?

10. Which toolbar is used to override the OSNAP selection?

Exercises

1. Draw the Mirror

2. Draw the Luggage Rack (Use Offset or Construction Line Offset, with OSNAP turned on to locate each feature)

3. Draw the Floor Lamp – 1/4″ Spokes start at 45° and are 90° apart. Hint: Use angled construction lines and offset them 1/8″ each side for the spokes.

4. Draw the Dresser – Knobs are located the same for each drawer (Use Offset or Construction Line Offset, with OSNAP turned on to locate each feature)

Chapter 4
Hotel Suite Project – Tutorial 1

Learning Objectives:

- **To create a drawing of a real-world application using AutoCAD®**
  - o **Create the plan view of the outside walls of the hotel suite**
- **To utilize and reinforce the use of the AutoCAD® commands learned in the previous chapters**

Hotel Suite Project

For our project, we will draw a hotel suite that will include a bedroom, bathroom, and a living room area. This project will utilize the majority of commands that will be covered throughout this book. The project will be broken down into multiple tutorials and each tutorial emphasizes commands covered in the preceding chapter.

The Hotel Suite

This tutorial covers the creation of the plan view of the hotel suite outside walls.

Commands & Techniques:

- Starting a new drawing
- Units
- Zoom - All
- Rectangle
- Offset
- Explode
- Construction Line – Offset
- Trim
- Extend
- Repeating commands by using the ↵ Enter key
- Erase
- Save

To help guide you through these tutorials, the following method is used to represent mouse and keyboard operations:

Bold font represents a keyboard operation.

Bold/Italic font in parenthesis represents a mouse operation.

Italic font represents AutoCAD® generated command line text.

Because the majority of the steps are repetitive, after the first several steps, the tutorial will not repeat every detail and prompt. When a new command is used, then the details will be given.

If you have already set up your mouse for customized right-click, everywhere the tutorial instructs you to press the ↵ Enter key, you can substitute that instruction with "right mouse-click".

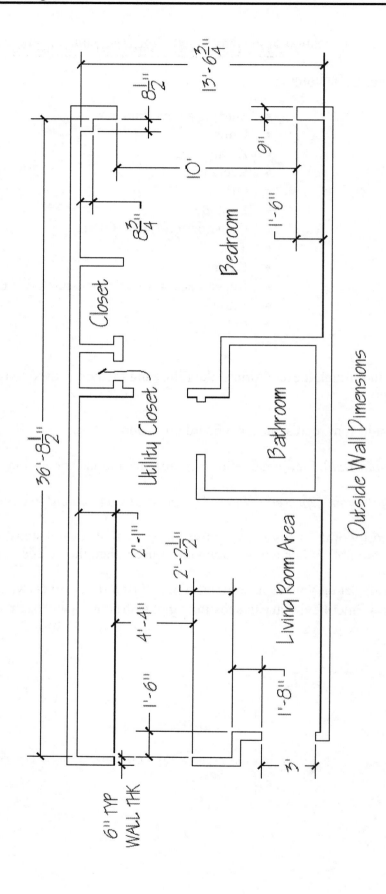

Create the basic shell of the suite

Basic Shell Dimensions

6" Thickness for Left, Top, and Bottom Walls

9" Thickness for Right Wall

The dashed lines are shown to illustrate that we can start this drawing by using rectangles.

- Before beginning, start up a new drawing, use the <u>Application Menu Browser</u> to select <u>Drawing Utilities</u>, and change the <u>Units</u> to **Architectural.**

1. **Change the units from decimal to feet-inches:**

    (Pick the Application Menu Browser, Pick Drawing Utilities, and Pick Units)

    (Change to Architectural Units in the Length Type: (upper left portion) pull-down arrow in the dialog box)

    (Pick OK to exit the dialog box)

2. **Create the inside walls using Rectangle:**

    (Pick Rectangle icon)

    RECTANG Specify first corner point or [Chamfer/Elevation/Fillet/Thickness/Width]: **(Pick a point on the screen, below and to the left of the center)**

    Use the Dimensions option to define the 36′8-1/2″ width and the 13′6-3/4″ height. AutoCAD® uses confusing definition for length and width; "length" = Horizontal direction, "width" = Vertical direction.

    > Note: when specifying Rectangle dimensions:
    > - Length is the horizontal direction
    > - Width is the vertical direction

    Specify other corner point or [Area/Dimensions/Rotation]: **d↵**
    Specify length for rectangles <0'-10">: **36'8-1/2** **↵**
    Specify width for rectangles <0'-10">: **13'6-3/4** **↵**
    Specify other corner point or [Area/Dimensions/Rotation]: **(Pick to the upper right of the 4 choices given)**

    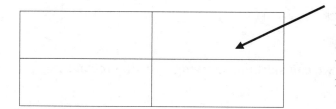

    As you move your cursor around the first corner point, four locations are available to choose. Pick the upper right location for the rectangle.

    (AutoCAD® will automatically end the Rectangle command)

When done, you will be left with only one rectangle, however it will not be seen in its entirety. That is because it is too big for the size of the view.

3. Change the screen zoom so that the entire drawing space is on the screen:

> _ **z** ↵
ZOOM
Specify corner of window, enter a scale factor (nX or nXP), or
ZOOM [All/Center/Dynamic/Extents/Previous/Scale/Window/Object] <real time>: **a** ↵
Regenerating model.
(AutoCAD® will automatically end the Zoom command)

When done, you will now be able to see the entire rectangle on your screen.

4. Use the Mouse Wheel to zoom out even further.

Your rectangle will appear even smaller. This will allow us to view more drawing space for when we offset the walls toward the outside.

5. Use the Offset command to draw the outside walls:

(Pick Offset icon)

OFFSET Current settings: Erase source=No Layer=Source OFFSETGAPTYPE=0
Specify offset distance or [Through] <Through>: **6** ↵

Specify point on side to offset or [Exit/Multiple/Undo] <Exit>: **(Pick the rectangle)**
Select object to offset or [Exit/Undo] <Exit>: **(Pick to the outside of the rectangle)**

Since no more offset lines are required, pressing the ⏎ Enter key will end the Offset command.

Select object to offset or <exit>: ⏎

When completed, your drawing will look like this.

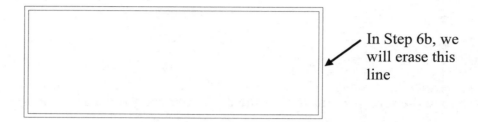

In Step 6b, we will erase this line

6. Draw the 9″ outside wall on the right side:

Our plan is to explode the rectangles first so that they become individual lines that we can work with. We will then be able to construct the thicker right wall.

6a. Prepare to draw the right outside wall by using the Explode command to convert the rectangles to lines:

(Pick the Explode icon)

EXPLODE Select objects: (Pick one of the rectangles) 1 found:
Select objects: (Pick the other rectangle) 1 found, 2 total

Since no more objects are to be exploded, pressing the ⏎ Enter key will end the Explode command.

Select objects: ⏎

6b. Erase the furthest right vertical line:

(Pick the Erase icon)

ERASE Select objects: (Pick the right vertical line) 1 found

Since no more objects are being erased, pressing the ⏎ Enter key will end the Erase command.

Select objects: ⏎

When completed,
your drawing will
look like this.

In step 6c, we will
create a construction
line offset from this
vertical line

6c. Construct the new right outside wall line for the 9″ thick wall:

(Pick the Construction Line icon)

XLINE Specify a point or [Hor/Ver/Ang/Bisect/Offset]: **o** ↵
Specify offset distance or [Through] <0'-6">: **9** ↵
Select a line object: (Pick the right vertical line)
Specify side to offset: (Pick anywhere to the right of the line you just selected)

Since no more offset construction lines are required, pressing the ↵ Enter key will end the
Offset command.

Select a line object: ↵

When you are done, your drawing should now look like this:

6d. Extend the horizontal lines to the new wall:

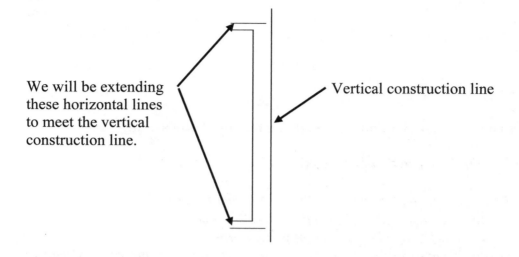

We will be extending these horizontal lines to meet the vertical construction line.

Vertical construction line

Remember that the Extend command is a two-part command; for the first part you pick the object (or objects) that you plan to extend to, for the second part you pick the objects to be extended.

(Pick the Extend icon)

Current settings: Projection=UCS, Edge=Extend
Select boundary edges ...
EXTEND *Select objects or <select all>: (Pick the vertical construction line) 1 found*

Since there are no more boundary lines, pressing the ⏎ Enter key will get you to the second part of the command.

Select objects: ⏎

Select object to extend or shift-select to trim or
[Fence/Crossing/Project/Edge/Undo]: (Pick the top horizontal line)

Select object to extend or shift-select to trim or
[Fence/Crossing/Project/Edge/Undo]: (Pick the bottom horizontal line)

> Note: the order in which you pick the lines to extend does not matter.

Since there are no more lines that need to be extended, pressing the ⏎ Enter key will end the Extend command.

Select object to extend or shift-select to trim or
[Fence/Crossing/Project/Edge/Undo]: ↵

When done, this portion of your drawing should look like this:

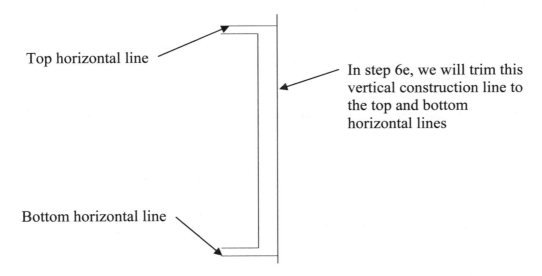

Top horizontal line

In step 6e, we will trim this vertical construction line to the top and bottom horizontal lines

Bottom horizontal line

6e. Trim the vertical construction line of the new wall to the top and bottom walls:

Remember that the Trim command is a two-part command (just as it was for the Extend command); for the first part you pick the object (or objects) that you plan to trim to (as if they were cutting knives), for the second part you pick the objects to be trimmed.

Since we just used the Extend command, the icon for the Extend command is now shown in the panel, and to access the Trim command, the pull-down arrow must be selected.

(Pick the Trim icon)

Current settings: Projection=UCS, Edge=Extend
Select cutting edges ...
***TRIM** Select objects or <select all>: **(Pick the top horizontal line)** 1 found*
*Select objects: **(Pick the bottom horizontal line)** 1 found, 2 total*

> Note: the order in which you pick the cutting edges does not matter.

Since there are no more cutting edges, pressing the ↵ Enter key will get you to the second part of the command.

Select objects: ↵

Select object to trim or shift-select to extend or
[Fence/Crossing/Project/Edge/eRase/Undo]: **(Pick the construction line in a location above the top horizontal line)**

Select object to trim or shift-select to extend or
[Fence/Crossing/Project/Edge/eRase/Undo]: **(Pick the construction line in a location below the bottom horizontal line)**

Note: the order in which you pick the location or lines to trim does not matter.

Since there is no more trimming required, pressing the ↵ Enter key will end the Trim command.

Select object to trim or shift-select to extend or
[Fence/Crossing/Project/Edge/eRase/Undo]: ↵

When you are done, your drawing should look like this:

7. Create the window opening in the bedroom

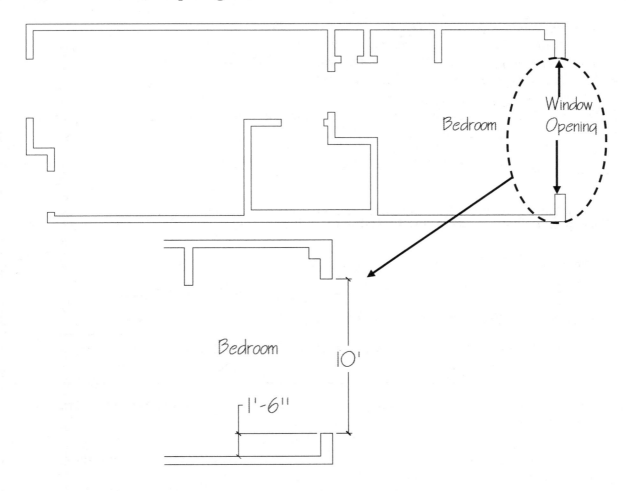

Our plan is to use both the **Construction Line – Offset** command and the **Offset** command to define the window opening. We will then trim the lines (and construction lines) to complete the window opening.

7a. Create a construction line offset from the bottom inside horizontal wall:

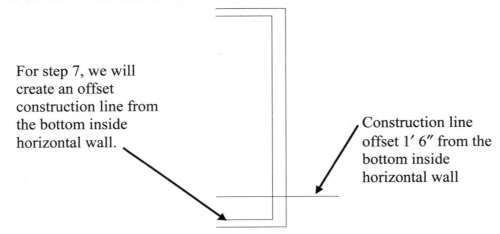

For step 7, we will create an offset construction line from the bottom inside horizontal wall.

Construction line offset 1′ 6″ from the bottom inside horizontal wall

(Pick the Construction Line icon)

XLINE Specify a point or [Hor/Ver/Ang/Bisect/Offset]: **o⏎**
Specify offset distance or [Through] <Through>: **1'6⏎**
Select a line object: (Pick the bottom inside horizontal line)
Specify side to offset: (Pick a location above the line you just selected)

Since we are not offsetting any more construction lines this distance, pressing the ⏎ Enter key will end the command.

Select a line object: ⏎
Command:

7b. Offset the new construction line to define the window size

(Pick the Offset icon)

Current settings: Erase source=No Layer=Source OFFSETGAPTYPE=0
OFFSET Specify offset distance or [Through/Erase/Layer] <1'-6">: **10'⏎**

> Note that the default value for the offset distance is the last value used for either the Offset command or the Construction Line Offset command

Select object to offset or [Exit/Undo] <Exit>: (Pick the horizontal construction line that you just created in step 7a)

Specify point on side to offset or [Exit/Multiple/Undo] <Exit>: (Pick a point anywhere above the horizontal construction line)

Since there are no more objects that we plan to offset, pressing the ⏎ Enter key will end the command.

Select object to offset or [Exit/Undo] <Exit>: ⏎

When you are done, your drawing should look like this:

In step 7c, we will trim the lines and construction lines to create the window opening.

7c. Use the Trim command to trim the lines and construction lines:

Using a crossing window will allow us to select multiple cutting edges with only two mouse clicks.

Remember: a crossing window goes from right to left, and any object that "crosses" that window, or is completely inside that window, is selected.

(Pick the Trim icon)

Current settings: Projection=UCS, Edge=Extend
Select cutting edges ...
TRIM *Select objects or <select all>:* **(Pick point at either location 1 or 1a)** *Specify opposite corner* **(Pick a point at either location 2 or 2a)** *4 found*

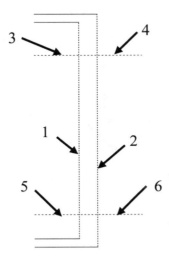

Since there are no more cutting edges, pressing the ↵ Enter key will get you to the second part of the command.

In the second part of the command, select the objects to be trimmed in the approximate locations shown (1-6). Note that the order in which you select the objects to be trimmed does not matter.

Select object to trim or shift-select to extend or [Fence/Crossing/Project/Edge/eRase/Undo]: ↵

The select object prompt will repeat until you press the ↵ Enter key to end the command.

When your are done trimming, your window opening will be complete.

8. Create the upper right corner of the bedroom

The upper right corner of the bedroom has a bump-out into the room because there is a structural column supporting the outside wall of the building. Our plan is to draw this bump-out by using the Offset and Trim commands.

Before beginning, you may want to use Zoom and Pan (using your mouse-wheel) to get a larger view of the upper right corner.

8a. Use the Offset command to offset the right inside wall line.

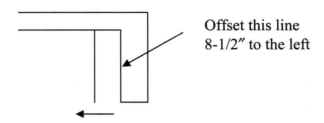

Offset this line
8-1/2″ to the left

8b. Press the ↵ Enter key to repeat the Offset command to offset the top inside wall line.

Offset this line
8-3/4″ down

8c. Use the Trim command to complete the corner

Use a crossing window to select the cutting edges:

Select the lines to be trimmed at the locations shown:

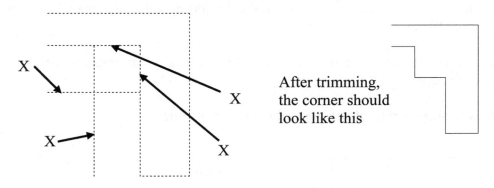

After trimming, the corner should look like this

8d. Use Zoom with the Extents option to view all your objects:

> _ **z** ↵
ZOOM
Specify corner of window, enter a scale factor (nX or nXP), or
ZOOM [All/Center/Dynamic/Extents/Previous/Scale/Window/Object] <real time>: **e**↵

In step 9, we will create a construction line offset from this wall line

9. Create the window opening in the living room area

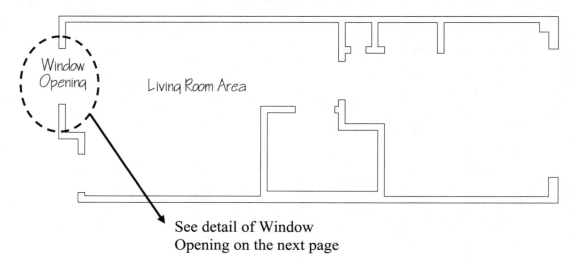

Window Opening

Living Room Area

See detail of Window Opening on the next page

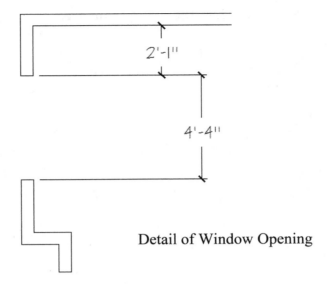

Detail of Window Opening

The steps required to create this window opening are very similar to the steps needed to create the bedroom window opening of step 7.

Our plan is to use both the Construction Line – Offset command and the Offset command to define the window opening. We will then trim the lines (and construction lines) to complete the window opening.

Before beginning, use the wheel mouse to zoom and pan to get a closer view of the window opening area that we will be working on.

9a. Create a Construction Line Offset 2′1″ from the upper inside wall

9b. Offset the construction line of step 9a 4′4″ down

9c. Use the Trim command to complete the window opening

Use the crossing window method to select the cutting edges, just like we did in step 7.

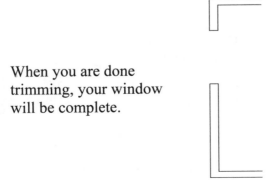

When you are done
trimming, your window
will be complete.

10. Create the entryway indentation into the living room area

10a. Create a Construction Line Offset 2′2-1/2″ down from line "A"

10b. Create a Construction Line Offset 1′6″ to the right of line "B"

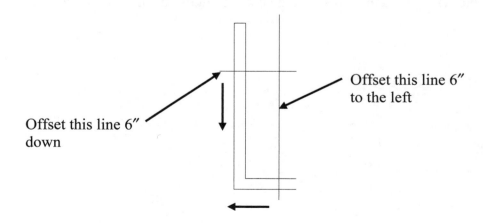

10c. Use the Offset command to Offset both construction lines 6″ each

After this step, this part of your drawing should look like this:

10d. Use the Trim command to trim construction lines

10e. Use the Erase command (if needed) to eliminate any extra lines

Depending on the order and location of the lines you picked during trimming, you may have some extra lines left over. Use the Erase command to eliminate them.

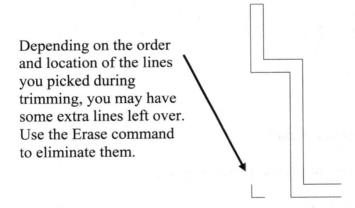

This is how much you have created so far! – Almost done!

11. Create the doorway opening into the living room area

Living Room Area

Doorway Opening

Line "C"

1'-8"

3'

11a. Offset line "C" 1'8" down

11b. Offset the line created in step 11a 3' down

11c. Use the Trim command to complete the doorway opening

Congratulations! You have now completed the basic shell of the hotel suite outside walls. Make sure to save your drawing so all that hard work won't be wasted!

12. Save the drawing

(Pick the Save icon)

After picking the Save icon, a dialog box will appear. If this is the first time saving, it will look similar to this:

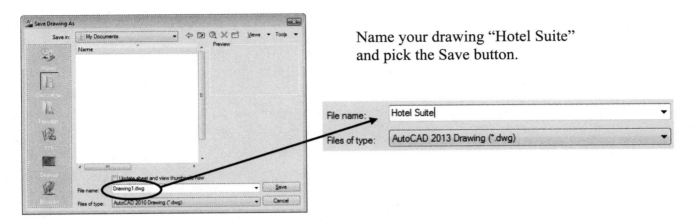

Name your drawing "Hotel Suite" and pick the Save button.

Notes:

Chapter 5
Commands – Set 2: Working with Your Drawing

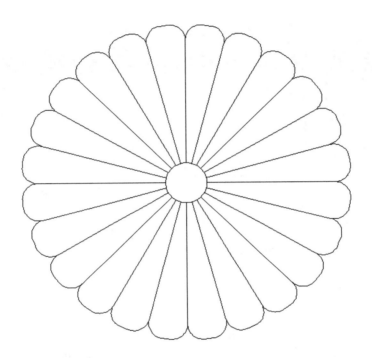

Learning Objectives:

- **Measure distances and angles between objects**
- **Measure the radius of an arc or a circle**
- **Obtain information about an object**
- **Create round, beveled or sharp corners**
- **Move, copy, rotate, and make a mirror image of objects**
- **Use the Array command to perform a 2-direction Copy for a Rectangular Array**
- **Use the Array command to perform a simultaneous Rotate and Copy for a Polar Array**

We are now able to draw basic objects very accurately. After you draw them, you may want to be able to verify that what you have drawn is as accurate as you believe you have drawn them. Fortunately, AutoCAD® has tools for getting information about the objects on your drawing.

Getting Information from Your Drawing

Two methods of getting information about the objects on your drawing are Measure and List. These commands can be found on the Home Tab. The Measure command is under the Utilities Panel and the List Command is under the Properties Panel.

Measure

The Measure command allows you to measure distance between points, the radius of a circular object, the angle between lines, and the area bounded by an object or shape defined by selected points. It can also measure volume of a 3D object, but only 2D is covered in this text.
The icon is a fly-out type of icon, with distance as the default icon on top. If you select other than the distance icon on the fly-out, that icon will now be displayed instead.

Distance

The Distance command is used to find the distance between two points, such as the endpoints of lines, center point of circle, etc. For accurate measurements, make sure you have OSNAP turned on.

Procedure:

Pick (left click): **Distance icon** from the Utilities Panel of the Home Tab.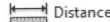

The command line prompts you with the following:

Enter an option [Distance/Radius/Angle/ARea/Volume] <Distance>: _distance
MEASUREGEOM *Specify first point:*

Select the first point of the two points you wish to find the distance between. For this example, pick point "A".

Example:

In this example, the line is 5″ long at a 45° angle

After you pick the first point, your command lines will look like the following:

Specify second point or [Multiple points]:

After you select the second point (point "B"), the requested information will be displayed above the active command line:

Distance = 0'-5", Angle in XY Plane = 45, Angle from XY Plane = 0
Delta X = 0'-3 9/16", Delta Y = 0'-3 9/16", Delta Z = 0'-0"

The command line will then prompt you to enter an option or continue to find distances:

Enter an option [Distance/Radius/Angle/ARea/Volume/eXit] <Distance>:

The command line will continue to prompt for more distance measurements, and allows you to choose other Measure Geometry options. If you have no more distances to measure, exit the command using the Escape key or typing **x** ↵ for eXit.

In addition to the command line, the information is also displayed on your screen when Dynamic Input is turned on. Dynamic Input switch is located on the Status Bar on the bottom of your screen.

Dynamic Input

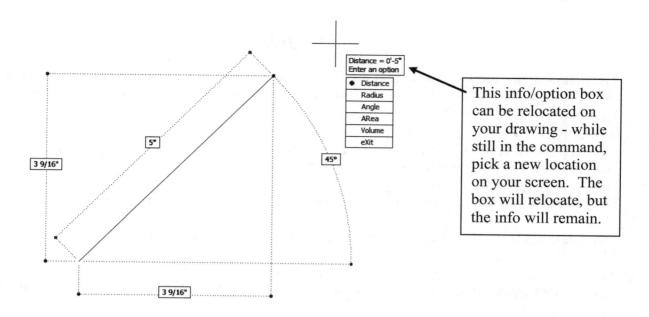

The information provided will give the distance between points, regardless of the angle between them. It will also give you the angle that would exist if a line were drawn between those points. Remember, angles are measured in a counterclockwise direction from the positive X-axis (Horizontal axis to the right of the origin). The order in which you select the points will make a difference in the angle given. For this example, point A was below point B. If the point B were selected first, the information would be as follows:

Distance = 0'-5", Angle in XY Plane = 225, Angle from XY Plane = 0
Delta X = -0'-3 9/16", Delta Y = -0'-3 9/16", Delta Z = 0'-0"

Notice that the angle of 225° is 180° more than 45° (45+180=225).

In addition to giving the direct distance between points, AutoCAD® also gives the distance from the first point to the second point in the X and Y (horizontal and vertical) directions (known as Delta X and Delta Y). Ignore the Z distance; this will always remain 0'-0" since we are drawing in 2-D.

Note that the first example (with the 45° angle) the X & Y values are positive because the direction from the first point to the second was to the right (+X) and up (+Y). For the second example (with the 225° angle) the X & Y values are negative because the direction from the first point to the second was to the left (-X) and down (-Y).

Radius

The Radius option allows you to measure the radius and diameter of an arc or circle.

<u>Procedure:</u>

Pick (left click): **Radius icon** from the Utilities Panel of the Home Tab.

Note that if the icon is not on the top of the Measure Fly-out list,
Pick the black triangle, and then move down the icon list to select the Radius icon.

The command line prompts you with the following:

Enter an option [Distance/Radius/Angle/ARea/Volume] <Distance>: _radius
***MEASUREGEOM** Select arc or circle:*

Pick the arc or circle you are interested in. For this example, pick the arc:

<u>Example:</u>

Radius = 0'-3 9/16"
Diameter = 0'-7 3/16"

Both the radius and diameter of the selected object are displayed on the command line and on the screen:

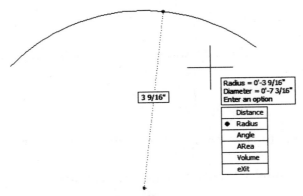

The command line will continue to prompt for more radial measurements, and allows you to choose other Measure Geometry options. If you have no more radii to measure, exit the command using the Escape key.

*Enter an option [Distance/Radius/Angle/ARea/Volume/eXit] <Radius>: *Cancel**

Angle

The Angle option allows you to measure the angle between lines, and between arc endpoints.

Procedure:

Pick (left click): **Angle icon** from the Utilities Panel of the Home Tab.

Note that if the icon is not on the top of the Measure Fly-out list, Pick the black triangle, and then move down the icon list to select the Angle icon.

The command line prompts you with the following:

Enter an option [Distance/Radius/Angle/ARea/Volume] <Distance>: _angle
MEASUREGEOM   *Select arc, circle, line, or <Specify vertex>:*

Select the first line of the two lines you wish to find the angle between.
For this example, pick "Line 1".

Example:

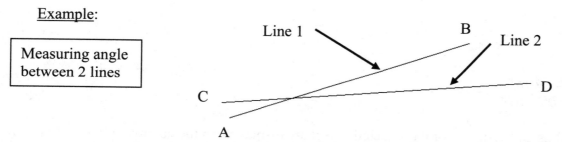

| Measuring angle between 2 lines |

After you pick the first line, your command lines will look like the following:

Select second line:

After you select the second line ("Line 2"), the requested information will be displayed above the active command line:

Angle = 14°

The command line will prompt you to enter an option or continue to find angles:

Enter an option [Distance/Radius/Angle/ARea/Volume/eXit] <Angle>:

The command line will continue to prompt for more angle measurements, and allows you to choose other Measure Geometry options. If you have no more distances to measure, exit the command using the Escape key.

In addition to the command line, the information is also displayed on your screen if Dynamic Input is turned on:

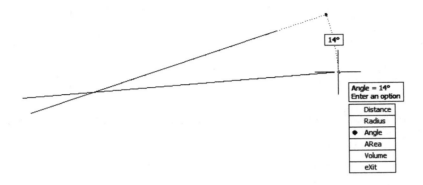

The angle that is measured may not have been the angle you desired. If you wanted the larger angle between the two, you could subtract the angle found from 180°. Alternatively, you could use the Vertex option. The vertex of an angle is the point where the two lines intersect.

Notice in the command line prompt, the vertex option is available:

Select arc, circle, line, or <Specify vertex>:

Simply press the ↵ Enter key to select this option. AutoCAD® will then prompt you with the following:

*Specify angle vertex: **(Pick the intersection of the two lines)***
*Specify first angle endpoint: **(Pick endpoint B of Line 1)***
*Specify second angle endpoint: **(Pick the endpoint C of Line 2)***
Angle = 166°
Enter an option [Distance/Radius/Angle/ARea/Volume/eXit] <Angle>:

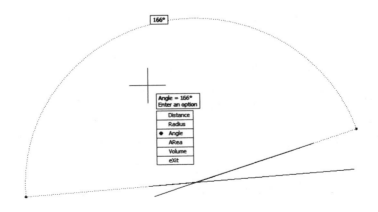

You can also measure the angle between arc endpoints. When prompted to select the object to measure the angle, simply pick the arc.

Example:

Measuring angle between arc endpoints

After selecting the arc, AutoCAD® will return the information on the command line and on your screen:

Angle = 104°
*Enter an option [Distance/Radius/Angle/ARea/Volume/eXit] <Angle>: *Cancel**

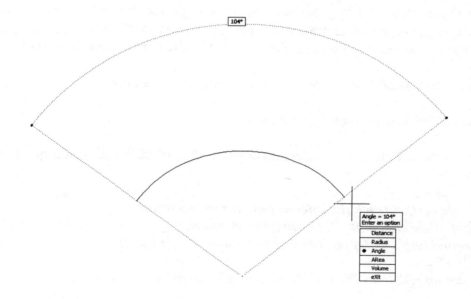

List

The List command is used to get information on an object, such as its length or location in the X-Y coordinates.

Procedure:

Pick (left click): Expand the Properties Panel of the Home Tab
                  Pick the **List icon** from the Inquiry toolbar.

LIST *Select objects:*
Pick the object you are interested in. The command line will continue to prompt for more objects until you press the ↵ Enter key:

Select objects:1 found
Select objects:

After you press the ↵ Enter key, the text window above the active command line will expand to provide you with the information about that object:

```
Command: _list
Select objects: 1 found
Select objects:
              LINE         Layer: "0"
                           Space: Model space
              Handle = 1c0
      from point, X=1'-2 1/4"  Y=0'-6 15/16"  Z=     0'-0"
        to point, X=1'-5 13/16"  Y=0'-10 1/2"  Z=     0'-0"
    Length =     0'-5",  Angle in XY Plane =       45
              Delta X =0'-3 9/16", Delta Y = 0'-3 9/16", Delta Z =     0'-0"
```

The information provided includes the type of object, (in this example, a line was selected), the layer that object is on, the start and end point in X & Y coordinates, the length, the angle it makes relative to the positive X-axis and the X & Y (Horizontal & Vertical) distance between the endpoints. For each object there is different information provided, depending on the type of object selected. Try this on your own and you will discover how useful this can be.

If more information is available than can be shown in the expanded text window, the active command line will prompt you to *Press ENTER to continue.*

Fillet – Creating Round or Square Corners

We have been able to make circles, lines, and construction lines. When we trim intersecting lines or construction lines, we end up with a sharp corner. There are many times that we want to make rounded corners. AutoCAD® has a command just for that and it is called Fillet.

But, in addition to making rounded corners, Fillet can also make square corners. This doesn't seem logical at first, but it can really come in handy. The square-corner Fillet is created by using a radius value of 0″. One major advantage of using the Fillet command for a square corner is to trim or extend lines simultaneously to complete an intersection.

The Fillet command allows you to connect two objects with an arc of a specified radius. The icon is on the Modify Panel of the Home Tab.

Procedure:

Pick (left click): **Fillet icon** from the Modify Panel of the Home Tab.

The command line prompts you with the following:

Current settings: Mode = TRIM, Radius = 0'-0″
FILLET *Select first object or [Undo/Polyline/Radius/Trim/Multiple]:*

Note that the "Current settings" shows you what the Mode and Radius values are set to. These can be changed prior to selecting your first object. Both Radius and Trim are options shown in the square brackets that you can choose. Type **r↵** to change the radius value. Type **t↵** to change trim value. If you have many fillets to create, you can choose the multiple option by typing **m↵** . If you do not choose multiple, then the Fillet command will end when you complete the single fillet.

Setting the Fillet Radius

The fillet radius is the radius of the arc that connects the two objects. If you set the fillet radius to 0″, filleted objects are trimmed or extended until they intersect, but no arc is created. Whatever value you choose for the fillet radius will be the default radius value the next time you select the Fillet command.

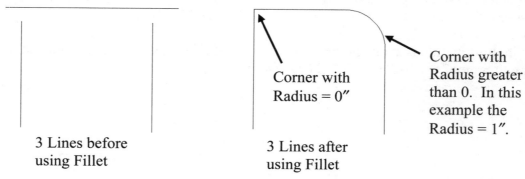

3 Lines before using Fillet

Corner with Radius = 0″

3 Lines after using Fillet

Corner with Radius greater than 0. In this example the Radius = 1″.

Trim Option

You can use the Trim option to specify whether the selected objects are trimmed or extended to the endpoints of the resulting arc or left unchanged. By default, all objects except circles, full ellipses, closed polylines, and splines (ellipses, polylines and splines will be discussed in a later chapter) are trimmed or extended when filleted.

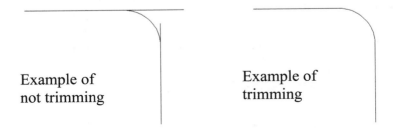

Example of
not trimming

Example of
trimming

Selecting Objects to Fillet

Select the first of two objects required to define a fillet, then, select the second object. The following will result (with *Mode = TRIM*):

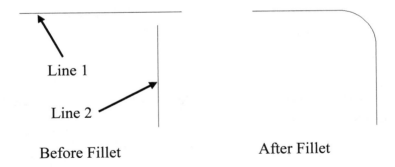

Line 1

Line 2

Before Fillet

After Fillet

Note that although the lines are labeled as "1" & "2", the order selected does not matter. As you will see later, what does matter is where you pick the objects to fillet.

If you select lines, arcs, or polylines, AutoCAD® extends or trims them until they intersect. Circles do not extend or trim with the Fillet command.

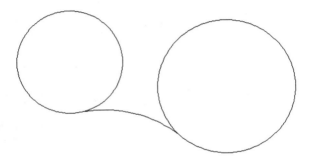

Importance of Pick Location

Depending on the locations you specify, more than one possible fillet can exist between the selected objects. Compare the selection points and resulting fillets for Lines "1" & "2":

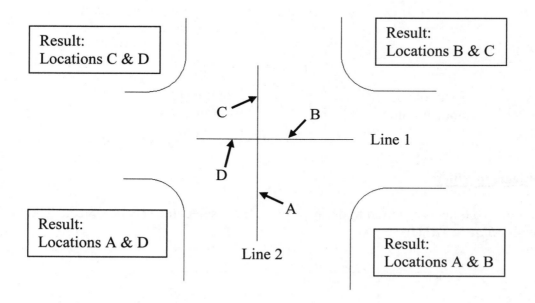

Result:
Locations C & D

Result:
Locations B & C

Line 1

Result:
Locations A & D

Line 2

Result:
Locations A & B

More than one fillet can exist between arcs and circles. AutoCAD® chooses the fillet with endpoints closest to the points you select.

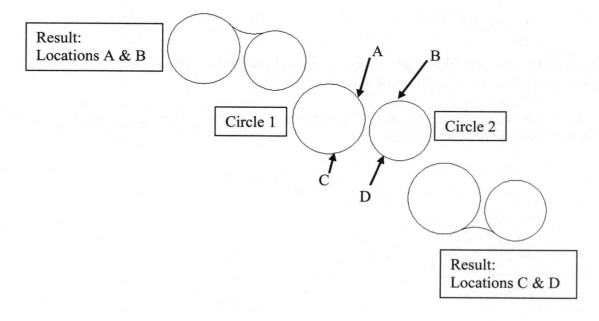

Result:
Locations A & B

Circle 1

Circle 2

Result:
Locations C & D

Recommendation:

Fillets are very useful for rounding inside or outside corners. With a radius value set to 0″, Fillets are extremely handy for closing a gap between two lines you want to have intersected with each other. For example, if you offset the inside wall line toward the outside to create the outside wall line, this will come up short. Extending would be difficult because the "boundary" also comes up short. Using Fillet will extend and trim both intersecting corner lines in one command.

Try it:

Let's try two examples: 1. Fillet between two lines
                            2. Fillet between a line and a circle

Example 1: Draw two lines anywhere on your screen. Make sure they are at least a couple inches long and are not parallel to each other:

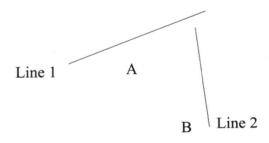

Now use the Fillet command to draw a 1″ Radius arc between them. Make sure that the Trim mode is on.

(Pick the Fillet icon)

Current settings: Mode = TRIM, Radius = 0'-0"
FILLET Select first object or [Undo/Polyline/Radius/Trim/Multiple]: **r⏎**
Specify fillet radius <0'-0">: **1⏎**
Select first object or [Undo/Polyline/Radius/Trim/Multiple]: **(Pick Line 1 near location A)**
Select second object or shift-select to apply corner or [Radius]: **(Pick Line 2 near location B)**

When you are done, your drawing will look like this:

Example 2: Draw a 2″ radius circle. Draw a line from the center of the circle to several inches beyond the circle:

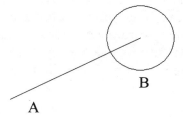

> The default value for the radius is 1″ because that was the value last used with this command from Example 1.

(Pick the Fillet icon)

Current settings: Mode = TRIM, Radius = 0'-1"
FILLET *Select first object or [Undo/Polyline/Radius/Trim/Multiple]:* ***(Pick the line near location A)***
Select second object or shift-select to apply corner or [Radius]: ***(Pick the circle near location B)***

When you are done, your drawing will look like this:

Chamfer – Creating Beveled Edges

The Chamfer command allows you to create a beveled edge of a specified angle or distance between two non-parallel lines. It is on the Modify Panel of the Home Tab. The icon is a fly-out type of icon, with fillet as the default icon on top. You must pick the black triangle to expand the fly-out to access the Chamfer icon. Once you select the Chamfer icon, it will be displayed on top.

Procedure:

Pick (left click): **Chamfer icon** from the Modify Panel of the Home Tab.

The command line prompts you with the following:

(TRIM mode) Current chamfer Dist1 = 0'-0", Dist2 = 0'-0"
CHAMFER *Select first line or [Undo/Polyline/Distance/Angle/Trim/mEthod/Multiple]:*

Note that the "Current chamfer" shows you what the Mode and Distance values are set to. These can be changed prior to selecting your first object. Both Distance and Trim are options shown in the square brackets that you can choose. Type **d↵** to change the distance value. Type **t↵** to change trim value. Type **a↵** to change the angle value. If you have many chamfers to create, you can choose the multiple option by typing **m↵** . If you do not choose multiple, then the Chamfer command will end when you complete the single chamfer.

Setting the Chamfer Distance

The chamfer distance is the starting and ending distance from the intersection of the two lines. If you set the chamfer distance to 0″, chamfered lines are trimmed or extended until they intersect, but no chamfer is created. Whatever value you choose for the chamfer distance will be the default distance values the next time you select the Chamfer command. You can also specify the chamfer angle. This option will require you to specify the distance to the first line and then the angle value.

Example of
Chamfer
with trim
option on

Other than the fact that this command creates angled corners (as opposed to rounded corners) it is very similar to the Fillet command. The trim option can be turned on and off, and the pick location is important. It is recommended that you understand the Fillet commands first and then explore the Chamfer command on your own.

Recommendation:

Chamfers are very useful for beveling corners. With a distance value set to 0″, chamfers are extremely handy for closing a gap between two lines you want to have intersected with each other. For example, if you offset the inside wall line to the outside to create the outside wall line, this will come up short. Extending would be difficult because the "boundary" also comes up short. Using Chamfer, with a distance value of 0″, will extend and trim both intersecting corner lines in one command.

Try it:

Usually (but not always) when you want to bevel an edge, it is between two perpendicular lines. For this example, let's draw a 45° beveled edge that begins 1″ from the corner.

Draw two perpendicular lines, each at least a few inches long, anywhere on your screen:

Line 1 — A — B — Line 2

(Pick the Chamfer icon)

(TRIM mode) Current chamfer Dist1 = 0'-0", Dist2 = 0'-0"
CHAMFER *Select first line or [Undo/Polyline/Distance/Angle/Trim/mEthod/Multiple]:* **a↵**
Specify chamfer length on the first line <0'-0">: **1↵**
Specify chamfer angle from the first line <0>: **45↵**
Select first line or [Undo/Polyline/Distance/Angle/Trim/mEthod/Multiple]: ***(Pick Line 1 near location A)***
Select second line or shift-select to apply corner: ***(Pick Line 2 near location B)***

When you are done, your drawing will look like this:

Manipulating Existing Objects

You can manipulate existing objects in the following ways:

- Move objects using the Move command.
- Make a copy of the objects to a new location using the Copy command
- Rotate objects using the Rotate command.
- Make a mirror image of objects using the Mirror command.
- Make a rectangular or polar array – combines Move with Copy, and Rotate with Copy

These commands are two part commands. The first part of the command requires you to select the objects. After the objects are selected, press the ↵ Enter key to get to the second part of the command. The second part of the command is further explained for each command in this document. The command icons are located on the Modify Panel of the Home Tab.

Move

Procedure:

Pick (left click): **Move icon** from the Modify Panel of the Home Tab.   ✛ Move

AutoCAD® will prompt you to select objects, and will continue to do so until you press the ↵ Enter key.

MOVE Select objects: **(Pick the objects you wish to move)**
Select objects: 1 found   (You can continue selecting as many objects you desire to move)
Select objects: ↵   (Pressing the ↵ Enter key will get you to the second part of the command)
Specify base point or [Displacement] <Displacement>: **(Pick a point to move "From")**
Specify second point or <use first point as displacement>: **(Pick a point to move "To")**
(AutoCAD® ends the command)

Try it:

Let's move an object to a specific location on the screen. For this example, let's move a circle to the intersection of two lines.

Before beginning this example, make sure that you have Object Snap (OSNAP) turned on with Center and Intersection selected.

Draw two intersecting lines anywhere on your screen. Draw a circle off to the side of these two lines. Now use the Move command to relocate the center of the circle to the intersection of the two lines:

(Pick the Move icon)

MOVE Select objects: (Pick the circle) 1 found

Specify base point or [Displacement] <Displacement>: (Pick the center of the circle – ensure that the AutoSnap marker shows that the center of the circle was found)

Specify second point or <use first point as displacement>: (Pick the intersection of the lines – ensure that the AutoSnap marker shows that the intersection was found)

When you are done, your drawing will look like this:

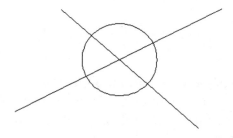

Copy

Procedure:

Pick (left click): **Copy icon** from the Modify Panel of the Home Tab.   Copy

AutoCAD® will prompt you to select objects, and will continue to do so until you press the ↵ Enter key.

COPY Select objects: **(Pick the objects you wish to copy)**
Select objects: 1 found   (You can continue selecting as many objects you desire to copy)
Select objects: ↵   (Pressing the ↵ Enter key will get you to the second part of the command)
Current settings: Copy mode = Multiple
Specify base point or [Displacement/mOde] <Displacement>: **(Pick a point to copy "From")**
Specify second point or [Array] <use first point as displacement>: **(Pick a point to copy "To")**
Specify second point or [Array/Exit/Undo] <Exit>: ↵

AutoCAD® allows you to continue to make multiple copies. Pressing the ↵ Enter key will end the command.

Try it:

Starting with the example from the Move command, add two more intersecting lines on your drawing:
(Make sure Object Snap is turned on with Center and Intersection selected)

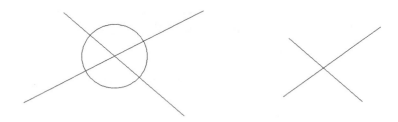

(Pick the Copy icon)

COPY Select objects: **(Pick the circle)** *1 found*
Select objects: ↵
Current settings: Copy mode = Multiple
Specify base point or [Displacement/mOde] <Displacement>: **(Pick the center of the circle)**
 Specify second point or [Array] <use first point as displacement>: **(Pick the intersection of the 2 new lines)**
Specify second point or [Exit/Undo] <Exit>: ↵

When you are done, your drawing will look like this:

Rotate

Procedure:

Pick (left click): **Rotate icon** from the Modify Panel of the Home Tab.

AutoCAD® will prompt you to select objects, and will continue to do so until you press the ↵ Enter key.

Current positive angle in UCS: ANGDIR=counterclockwise ANGBASE=0
ROTATE *Select objects: (Pick the objects you wish to rotate)*
Select objects: 1 found   (You can continue selecting as many objects you desire to rotate)

Select objects: ↵   (Pressing the ↵ Enter key will get you to the second part of the command)
Specify base point: (Pick a point to rotate about)
                    (The objects begin to rotate with movement of the cursor)
Specify rotation angle or [Reference]: **45** ↵
                    (Key in a desired angle. Remember, the angle is measured in a counterclockwise direction. Alternatively, you can Pick a point to define the angle)
(AutoCAD® ends the command)

Try it:

Starting with the example of the Copy command, let's rotate the right circle 90° about the left circle.

(Pick the Rotate icon)
Current positive angle in UCS: ANGDIR=counterclockwise ANGBASE=0
***ROTATE** Select objects: (**Pick the right circle**) 1 found*
Select objects: ↵
*Specify base point: (**Pick the center of the left circle**)*
Specify rotation angle or [Copy/Reference] <0>: **90**↵

When you are done, your drawing will look like this:

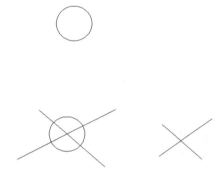

Notice that we have entered a specific angle to rotate these objects. You can use the Reference option to rotate objects without entering a specific value. Instead, you select locations on the drawing as a reference for the angle.

Example:

Rotate the circle to the horizontal line:

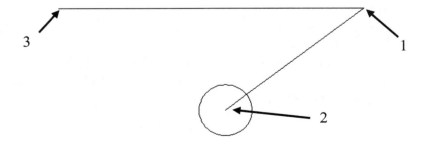

(Pick the Rotate icon)
Current positive angle in UCS: ANGDIR=counterclockwise ANGBASE=0
***ROTATE** Select objects: **(Pick the circle)** 1 found*
Select objects: ↵
*Specify base point: **(Pick point 1)***
*Specify rotation angle or [Copy/Reference] <0>: **r**↵*
*Specify the reference angle <0>: **(Pick point 1)** Specify second point: **(Pick point 2)***
*Specify the new angle or [Points] <0>: **(Pick point 3)***

The circle has rotated through an angle to match the horizontal line. By using the Reference option, we did not need to know the value of the angle.

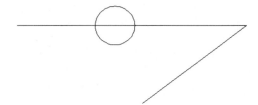

Mirror

Prior to using the Mirror command, it is a good idea to have a pre-defined line to mirror about. AutoCAD® looks for two points that define a mirror line.

Procedure:

Pick (left click): **Mirror icon** from the Modify Panel of the Home Tab.   Mirror

AutoCAD® will prompt you to select objects, and will continue to do so until you press the Enter ↵ key.

MIRROR** Select objects: **[Pick the objects you wish to mirror]
Select objects: 1 found   (You can continue selecting as many objects you desire to mirror)
Select objects: ↵   (Pressing the Enter ↵ key will get you to the second part of the command)
Specify first point of mirror line:
                                  (If you have a pre-determined line you want to mirror about, then select the first endpoint of that line. A mirror image of the objects will follow your cursor until the second mirror line is defined)
Specify first point of mirror line: Specify second point of mirror line: **(Select the second endpoint of the pre-defined line)**   (The mirror image will temporarily disappear)

Delete source objects? [Yes/No] <N>:

> (Type "**y**" if you wish to delete the original objects. Otherwise, accept the default value of "**n**" by pressing the ↵ Enter key. This will leave the original objects in place and you will have a mirrored-copy of your objects)

(AutoCAD® ends the command)

Try it:

Starting with the example from the Rotate command, let's make a mirror image of what we have drawn.

Start by drawing a line that is nearly vertical towards the left side of the objects on the screen:

(Pick the Mirror icon)

MIRROR *Select objects:* **(Pick the objects that are to the right of the line using a selection window)**
 Specify opposite corner: 6 found
Select objects: ↵
Specify first point of mirror line: **(Pick the endpoint of the nearly-vertical line)**
Specify second point of mirror line: **(Pick the other endpoint of the nearly-vertical line)**
Erase source objects? [Yes/No] <N>: ↵

When you are done, your drawing will look like this:

Recommendation:

These commands are very powerful and allow you to complete a drawing much faster than doing it by hand. There are additional options for these commands that are not covered here. It is left to the student to learn more about these options by exploring or using the online help. To rotate while copying, or move while copying, use the Array command.

Array Commands

The Array commands allow you to copy while rotating or moving. After the array is created, it is treated as one object. The Array command icon is a fly-out type of icon (as indicated with the black triangle in the lower right-hand corner), located on the Modify Panel of the Home Tab. There are three icons that occupy the same position on the toolbar, which are stacked on top of each other. The most recently used icon is one displayed on the top. This chapter will cover the Rectangular and Polar Array commands.

 Rectangular Array   □ □
□   □ Polar Array
□ □

Rectangular Array

The Rectangular Array will allow you to make copies of the original object in rows and columns. The quantity of rows is the count in the vertical direction. The quantity of columns is the count in the horizontal direction

Procedure:

Pick (left click): **Rectangular Array icon** from the
                   Modify Panel of the Home Tab.

ARRAYRECT Select objects: **(Pick the objects that will be used for the array)**
Select objects: 1 found   (AutoCAD® will allow you to continue picking objects until you press
                   the ↵ Enter key)
Select objects: ↵
Type = Rectangular Associative = Yes
Select grip to edit array or
[ASsociative/Basepoint/COUnt/Spacing/COLumns/Rows/Levels/eXit]<eXit>:

You will get immediate visual feedback. In addition to having multiple rows and columns of the objects selected, grips will also appear. Each grip has a different function.

Rectangular Grips
Lower Left: Moves the entire array.
Upper Right: Adjusts row and column count
Triangular Grips
Left Column
Top: Adjusts row count
Bottom: Adjusts row spacing
Lower Row
Right: Adjusts column count
Left: Adjusts column spacing

To use the grips, Pick on the grip of your choice (left click and release). The grips will disappear. As you move the cursor to a new position, it will appear as if a line is "rubber banding" from the original grip location to the new location. This is not a line; it is visual aid to show the old and new locations of the grip selected.
You will get visual feed back of the change you are making. When you are satisfied, left click again to choose the new grip position.

Using the grips for adjusting row and column count, as well as repositioning the array, is easy to control.

Count Option

Although the visual feedback of rows and columns comes in handy, there are occasions when you want a large enough quantity that you don't want to count them on the screen as they appear with cursor movement. Using the Count option allows you to type in the value you desire for each. After you have chosen the objects for the array, use the Count option of the command by pressing the ↲ Enter key.

Select grip to edit array or [ASsociative/Base point/COUnt/Spacing/COLumns/Rows/Levels/eXit]<eXit>: **cou↲**

Enter the number of columns or [Expression] <4>:

Enter the number of rows or [Expression] <4>:Key in a value for the number of rows (vertical direction), followed by pressing the ↲ Enter key.

Enter number of columns or [Expression] <X>:

Key in a value for the number of columns (horizontal direction), followed by pressing the ↲ Enter key.

The Rectangular Array command will then prompt for the spacing as described earlier.

Spacing Option

You will most likely want to control the spacing value. Rather than simply picking on the screen, you can specify the distance. After you have chosen the number of rows and columns, use the Spacing option of the command:

Select grip to edit array or [ASsociative/Base point/COUnt/Spacing/COLumns/Rows/Levels/eXit]<eXit>: **s↲**

As an example, if we want to space our rows and columns 1" apart, we would type in the value when prompted. The prompt will include a default value in the angled brackets. This value will be different each time.

Specify the distance between columns or [Unit cell] < X-' XX">:
Key in a specified distance you want between columns, followed by pressing the ⏎ Enter key.

Specify the distance between rows < X-' XX">:
Key in a specified distance you want between rows, followed by pressing the ⏎ Enter key.

When you are finished specifying distances between columns and rows, the prompt will return to the original choices.

Select grip to edit array or [ASsociative/Base point/COUnt/Spacing/COLumns/Rows/Levels/eXit]<eXit>:

Try it:

Let's draw a 6 X 6 pattern of 1" squares that are 1-1/8" apart (this will put a 1/8" gap between the squares):

First, draw the 1" square anywhere on the screen (use the Rectangle command):

(Pick the Rectangular Array command)

ARRAYRECT *Select objects:* **(Pick the square)**
Select objects: 1 found ⏎

Type = Rectangular Associative = Yes
Select grip to edit array or [ASsociative/Base point/COUnt/Spacing/COLumns/Rows/Levels/eXit]<eXit>: **cou⏎**

Enter the number of columns or [Expression] <4>: **6⏎**
Enter the number of rows or [Expression] <3>: **6⏎**

As an alternative: Pick a point in a direction away from the objects until you see 6 rows and 6 columns of squares.

The original prompt returns to the command line. Adjust the spacing by choosing that option:

Select grip to edit array or [ASsociative/Base point/COUnt/Spacing/COLumns/Rows/Levels/eXit]<eXit>: **s⏎**

Specify the distance between columns or [Unit cell] <1 1/2">: **1-1/8⏎**
Specify the distance between rows <1 1/2">: **1-1/8⏎**

When the original prompt returns, press the Enter ⏎ key to exit the command.

Select grip to edit array or [ASsociative/Base point/COUnt/Spacing/COLumns/Rows/Levels/eXit]<eXit>: **⏎**

When you are done, your drawing will look like this:

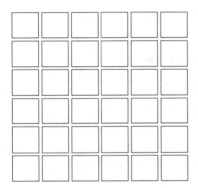

Note that these 36 squares are treated as one object identified as an Array. To make these individual squares, use the Explode command.

Polar Array

The Polar Array will allow you to make copies of the original object rotated about a point.

Procedure:

Pick (left click): **Polar Array icon** from the
Modify Panel of the Home Tab.

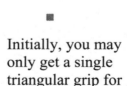 Polar Array

ARRAYPOLAR *Select objects:* ***(Pick the objects that will be used for the array)***

Select objects: 1 found   (AutoCAD® will allow you to continue picking objects until you press the ↵ Enter key)

Select objects: ↵

Type = Polar Associative = Yes
Specify center point of array or [Base point/Axis of rotation]:

(Pick a point that the selected objects will rotate about)

Select grip to edit array or [ASsociative/Base point/Items/Angle between/Fill angle/ROWs/Levels/ROTate items/eXit]<eXit>:

You will get immediate visual feedback. In addition to having multiple copies of the objects selected, grips will also appear. Each grip has a different function.

Initially, you may only get a single triangular grip for angle between items.	**Rectangular Grips** Normal Square: Moves the entire array. Angled Square: Stretches the radial distance from the base point **Triangular Grips** 1st - Changes the angle between items 2nd - Changes item count

After you select the first triangular grip, a second one may appear for item count.

To use the grips, Pick on the grip of your choice (left click and release). The grips will disappear. As you move the cursor to a new position, it will appear as if a line is "rubber banding" from the original grip location to the new location. This is not a line; it is visual aid to show the old and new locations of the grip selected.
You will get visual feed back of the change you are making. When you are satisfied, left click again to choose the new grip position.

You may have a specific number of items that must fill a certain angle, or you may know the angle between items that you want. This command allows you to define the array in multiple ways. We will just cover the fill angle and the number of items.

If you want to fill a full circle, use the Fill option with an angle of 360. Note that the fill angle of 360 is the default fill angle, so you typically do not need this option if you plan to fill a full circle.

Specify the angle to fill (+=ccw, -=cw) or [EXpression] <360>:

If you know the number of items, use the Items option.

Enter number of items in array or [Expression] <X>:

Pressing the ↵ Enter key will end the command.

Try it:

Let's draw the 4 flower petals shown:

First we will draw a single flower petal, and then we will rotate and copy that petal by using the Polar Array command. The petal is a 1″ radius circle drawn at the intersection of a line and a 2″ radius circle.

Start by drawing a 2″ radius circle anywhere on your screen. Now draw a horizontal construction line through the center of the circle. At the right intersection of the construction line and the 2″ radius circle, draw a 1″ radius circle.

At this point, your drawing will look like this:

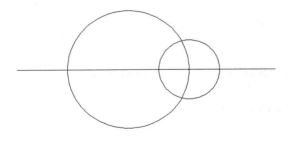

Now draw two lines that start from the center of the 2″ radius circle and ending tangent to the 1″ radius circle:

(If you do not have OSNAP set to Tangent, you can use the Object Snap toolbar to snap to the tangent of the circle when the Line command is prompting for the second endpoint

Start of Line:
Use Snap to Center

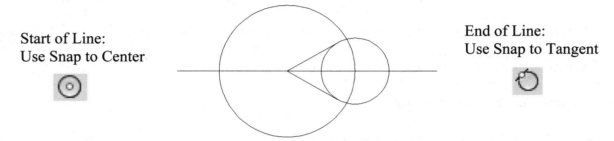

End of Line:
Use Snap to Tangent

Use the Trim command to trim away the small portion of the 1″ radius circle:

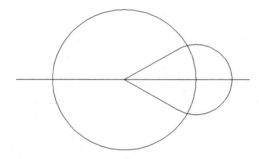

Now that we have the first petal drawn, we can use the Polar Array command to copy it around the center of the 2″ radius circle.

(Pick the Polar Array command)

ARRAYPOLAR *Select objects:*

(Pick the two lines and the semi-circle)

Select objects: 1 found
Select objects: 1 found, 2 total
Select objects: 1 found, 3 total
Select objects: ↵

Type = Polar Associative = Yes
Specify center point of array or [Base point/Axis of rotation]:

(Pick the Center of the 2″radius circle)

Use the Items option to specify the number of petals to be 4:

Select grip to edit array or [ASsociative/Base point/Items/Angle between/Fill angle/ROWs/Levels/ROTate items/eXit]<eXit>: **i↵**

Enter number of items in array or [Expression] <6>: **4↵**

Since 360 was the default value for angle to fill, we do not need to specify the fill angle. We can exit the command by pressing the ↵ Enter key.

When you are done, your drawing will look like this:

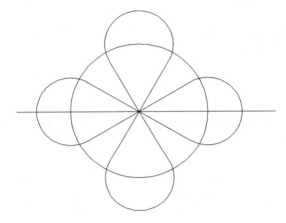

You can erase the 2″ radius circle and the construction line to get the final drawing of the flower:

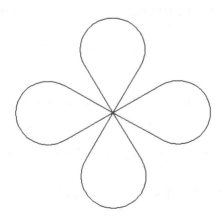

Summary

In this chapter you have learned to:

- Recognize and understand a Fly-out icon
- Measure distances between points
- Measure the radius and diameter of an arc or circle
- Measure the angle between lines
- Obtain all the information available about an object
- Move, copy, rotate, and mirror objects
- Create a rectangular pattern of objects
- Create a circular pattern of objects

Review Questions

1. What is a Fly-out style icon?

2. On the Inquiry toolbar, you see the Distance command but not the Angle command. Where is it and how do you get to it?

3. When using the Distance command, AutoCAD® will give you the distance between two points. What other information will AutoCAD® provide?

4. The information about an object will show up in your command line and where else?

5. When using either the Fillet or Chamfer commands, does the order in which you pick the objects matter? Does the location matter?

6. If Fillets are used to make rounded corners, how can you use it to make a sharp corner?

7. Why would you use Fillet to make sharp corners instead of using either the Trim or Extend commands?

8. When using the Move, Copy, or Rotate commands, what is a base point that AutoCAD® is prompting for?

9. Prior to using the Mirror command, what should you have prepared in advance?

10. Which commands are used for making either rectangular or circular patterns?

Exercises

1. Draw the conference room. The doors are 1-3/4" thick.

2. Draw the 3′ x 1-3/4″ door and door swing. Make mirrored-copies of the door. Copy and rotate the mirrored-copies 90°.

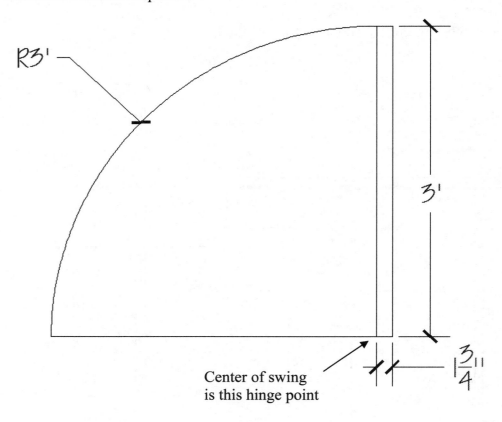

R3′

3′

Center of swing
is this hinge point

1 3/4″

Door & Swing dimensions

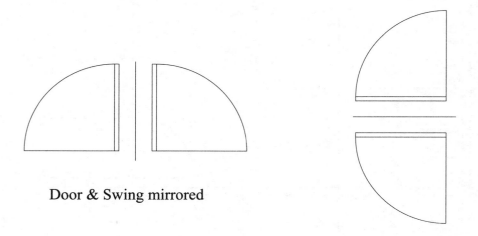

Door & Swing mirrored

Door & Swing rotated 90° after mirroring

3. Draw the Conference Chair.

4. Draw the tile pattern. The spacing between tiles is 1/16″.

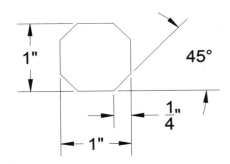

Draw the single tile shown and use a Rectangular Array with spacing set to 1-1/16″ for both columns and rows.

5. Draw the Spoke Chair.

Hint: Draw 1 spoke and use the Polar Array to copy
them around the chair – 10 places within 180°

6. Draw the medallion.

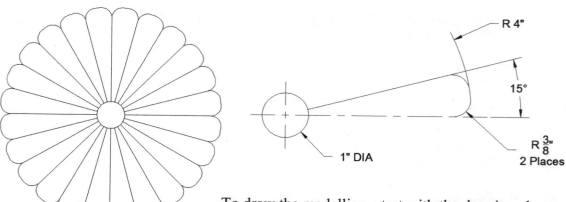

To draw the medallion, start with the drawing above.
Use a Polar Array to rotate and copy the objects. Do
not include the 1″ diameter circle or the centerlines
when you select the objects for the array.

Chapter 6
Hotel Suite Project – Tutorial 2

Learning Objectives:

- **To continue creating a drawing of a real-world application of AutoCAD®**
  - Create the plan view of the bathroom and closet walls of the hotel suite
  - Create the doors and windows of the suite
- **To utilize and reinforce the use of the AutoCAD® commands learned in the previous chapters**

This tutorial builds on Tutorial 1 found in Chapter 4. We will create the bathroom and closet walls of the hotel suite. When you are finished with this tutorial, all the walls of the plan view of the hotel suite will be completed.

The drawing methods used to complete the walls are very similar to those used for tutorial 1.

Commands & Techniques:

- Opening an existing drawing
- Zoom - All
- Rectangle
- Offset
- Explode
- Construction Line – Offset & Horizontal
- Trim
- Erase
- Fillet
- Repeating commands by using the ↵ Enter key
- Object Snap – Endpoint
- Distance
- Copy
- Rotate
- Mirror
- Move
- Save

Create the Bathroom Walls

Bathroom Dimensions

- To begin, we will call up the drawing that you created in Tutorial 1.

1. **Use the Open icon to open the Hotel Suite drawing.**

   (Pick the Open icon)

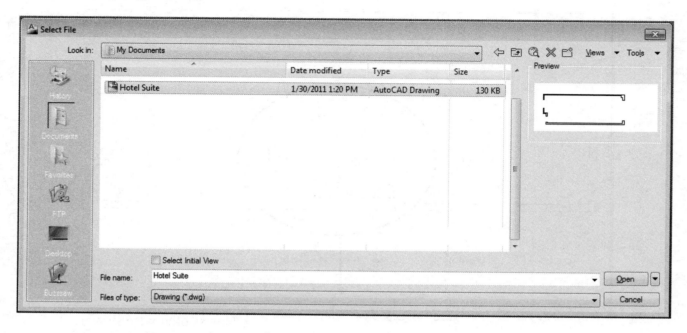

   (Pick the file icon)

The preview pane shows you a thumbnail representation of the drawing. This makes it easy to determine if you are about to open the correct drawing.

   (Pick Open)

Your drawing should now appear on your computer screen. Zoom and Pan to the area of the drawing that will become the bathroom.

2. Create construction lines for the right and left vertical walls

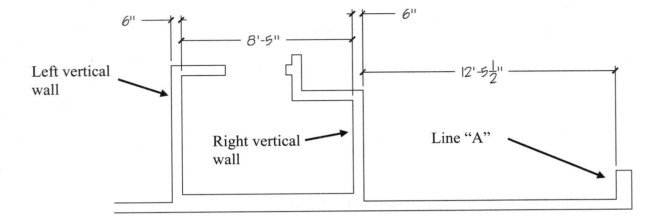

2a. Create a Construction Line Offset 12′5-1/2″ from line "A"

Use the **Construction Line** command with the **Offset** option

2b. Offset the construction line of step 2a 6″ to create the wall thickness

Use the **Offset** command.

2c. Offset the construction line of step 2b 8′5″ to create the inside left vertical wall line

Press the ↵ Enter key to repeat the **Offset** command

2d. Offset the construction line of step 2c 6″ to create the wall thickness

When you are
done, your
drawing should
look like this.

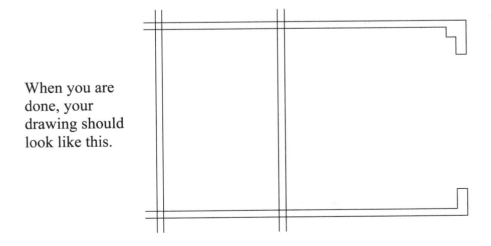

3. Create the lower horizontal wall

Line "B"

$4\frac{3}{4}''$

3a. Offset line "B" 4-3/4″ to create the wall thickness

3b. Use the Trim command to complete the lower horizontal wall

Take advantage of using a crossing window to select your cutting edges.

Remember, if during trimming you have extra lines as a result of the location and order in which you picked the lines to trim, use the Erase command to eliminate them.

When you are done, your drawing should look like this:

4. Create the upper left horizontal wall

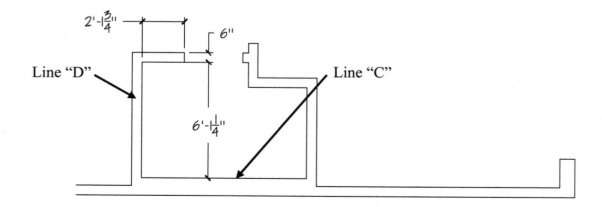

$2'-1\frac{3}{4}''$

$6''$

Line "D"

Line "C"

$6'-1\frac{1}{4}''$

4a. Offset line "C" 6′1-1/4″ up to create the inside line of the upper left horizontal wall

4b. Offset the line created in step 4a 6″ up to create the wall thickness

4c. Offset line "D" 2′1-3/4″ to the right

So far, your drawing should look like this:

Use Zoom and Pan
to get a closer view
of this area.

To continue on, it may be easier to complete the wall by getting a closer view. Use the wheel mouse to Zoom and Pan to do this.

A close-up view
of the upper left
wall area

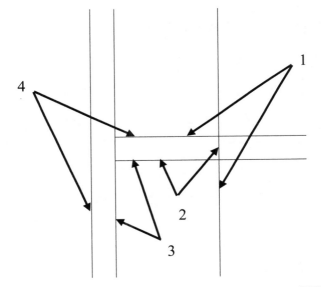

4d. Use the Fillet command to close out the wall lines

If the Radius is not set to 0′-0″ press **r↵** *and change the value by keying* **0↵**

(Pick the Fillet icon)

Current settings: Mode = TRIM, Radius = 0′-0″
FILLET *Select first object or [Undo/Polyline/Radius/Trim/Multiple]:*
(Pick one of the lines at location marked 1)
Select second object or shift-select to apply corner:
(Pick the other line at location marked 1)

The Fillet command will end after the second line is picked and it will trim both lines.

Both lines are
trimmed and the
corner is square.

4e. Continue using the Fillet command to trim the lines at locations marked 2, 3 & 4

Remember, you can quickly repeat the Fillet command by pressing the ↵ Enter key.

Now that you have used the Trim and/or Extend commands and the Fillet command, you may notice that the Fillet command comes in very handy. I find the Fillet command to be fewer steps. The Trim command is still needed when you want to remove a mid-section of an object.

When you are done, your drawing should look like this:

5. Create the upper right horizontal and vertical walls

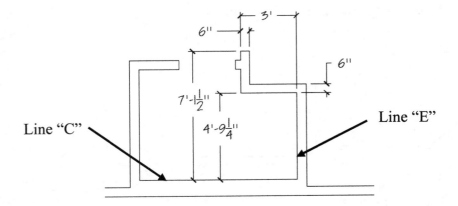

Line "C"

Line "E"

5a. Offset line "C" 4′9-1/4″ up to create the inside wall line

5b. Offset the line you created in step 5a 6″ up to create the wall thickness

5c. Offset line "E" 3′ to the left

5d. Offset the line you created in step 5c 6″ to the right to create the wall thickness

So far, your drawing should look like this:

Use Zoom and Pan to get
a closer view of this area

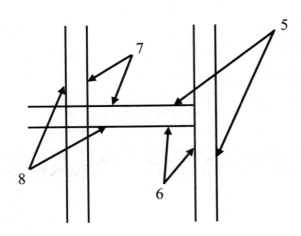

5e. Use the Fillet command to trim the lines at locations marked 5, 6,7, & 8

When you are done, your drawing should look like this:

Line "C"

5f. Offset line "C" 7′ 1-1/2″ up

5g. Use the Fillet command to close out the corners of the wall

6. Create the door opening

For the door opening, a small piece of horizontal wall needs to be added. This is in-line with the left horizontal wall.

9

10

Line "F"

6a. Turn on Object Snap Endpoint

Right-Click on the
Object Snap switch

Command:

23'-1 1/8", 7'-2 5/16" , 0'-0"

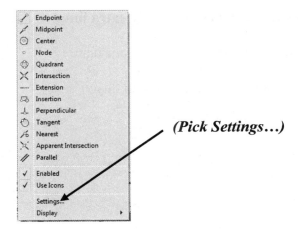

(Pick Settings...)

When the Drafting Settings dialog box appears, left-click the check-box next to Endpoint and Object Snap On if they are not already checked off. Pick OK to close the dialog box.

6b. Create Horizontal Construction Lines to define the right side of the door opening

(Pick the Construction Line icon)

XLINE Specify a point or [Hor/Ver/Ang/Bisect/Offset]: **h** ↵
Specify through point: (Pick the endpoint at location marked 9)
Specify through point: (Pick the endpoint at location marked 10)
Specify through point: ↵

6c. Offset line "F" 3′ to the right to define the door opening

6d. Use the Trim command to complete the opening

6e. Use the Erase command if needed to eliminate any extra lines

This now completes the bathroom portion of the floor plan.

When you are done, your drawing should look like this:

Make sure to save your drawing. Next, we will add the closet wall lines.

Create the Closet Walls

Closet Dimensions

7. Create the right vertical wall of the right closet

7a. Create a Construction Line Offset 7′3″ from line "A"

7b. Offset the construction line of step 7a 6″ to create the wall thickness

7c. Offset line "B" 2′5″ down to create the wall length

7d. Use the Trim command to complete the wall

When you are done, your drawing should look like this.

8. Create the left wall of the right closet

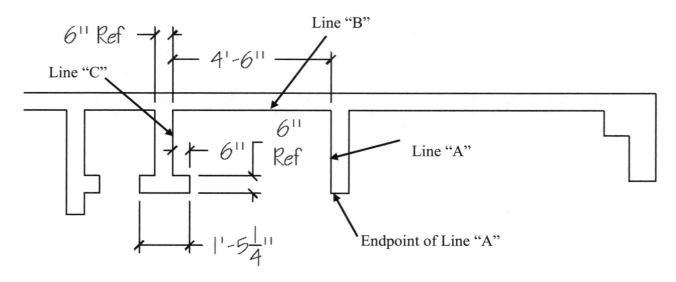

8a. Offset line "A" 4′6″ to the left

8b. Offset the line created in step 8a 6″ to the left

8c. Use the Trim command to trim line "B"

8d. Create a Horizontal Construction Line from the endpoint of line "A"

8e. Offset 6″ - the horizontal construction line upward and line "C" to the right

8f. Repeat the Offset command and Offset the vertical line created in step 8e 1′5-1/4″ to the left

8g. Use the Fillet command with a 0″ radius to finish the corners shown

Use Fillet to complete these corners

When you are
done, your
drawing should
look like this.

8h. Use the Trim command to clean up the remaining lines

When you are
done, your
drawing should
look like this.

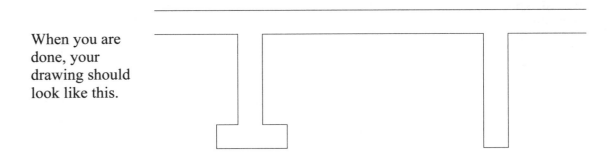

9. Create the left wall of the utility closet

9a. Create Vertical Construction Lines passing through endpoints "1" and "2"

9b. Use the Trim command to complete the top part of the left utility closet wall

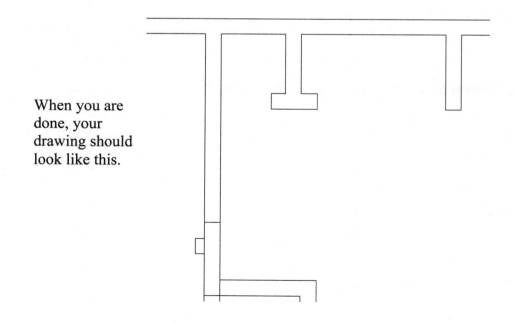

When you are done, your drawing should look like this.

10. Create the door opening for the bedroom

    10a. Offset line "A" 3′ up

    10b. Use the Trim command to complete the door opening

When you are
done, your
drawing should
look like this.

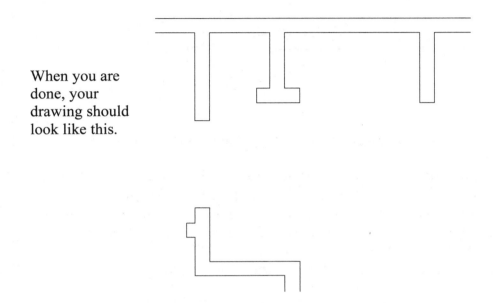

11. Finish the utility closet structure

    11a. Create Horizontal Construction Lines through endpoints "3" and "4"

    11b. Offset line "B" 1′1-1/2″ to the left

    11c. Use the Trim command to complete the structure

When you are
done, your
drawing should
look like this.

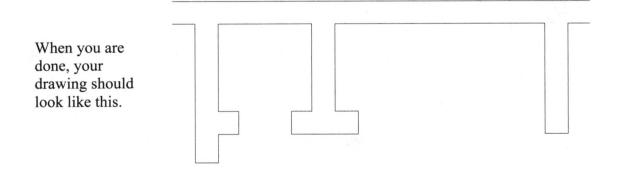

12. Confirm the reference dimensions for lines "A", "B", and "C"

12a. Pick the Distance command from the Utilities Panel of the Home Tab

Enter an option [Distance/Radius/Angle/ARea/Volume] <Distance>: _distance
MEASUREGEOM *Specify first point:* **(Pick one endpoint of line "A")**
Specify second point or [Multiple points]: **(Pick the other endpoint of line "A")**
Distance = 3'-0 1/2", Angle in XY Plane = 90, Angle from XY Plane = 0
Delta X = 0'-0", Delta Y = -3'-0 1/2",   Delta Z = 0'-0"
Enter an option [Distance/Radius/Angle/ARea/Volume/eXit] <Distance>:

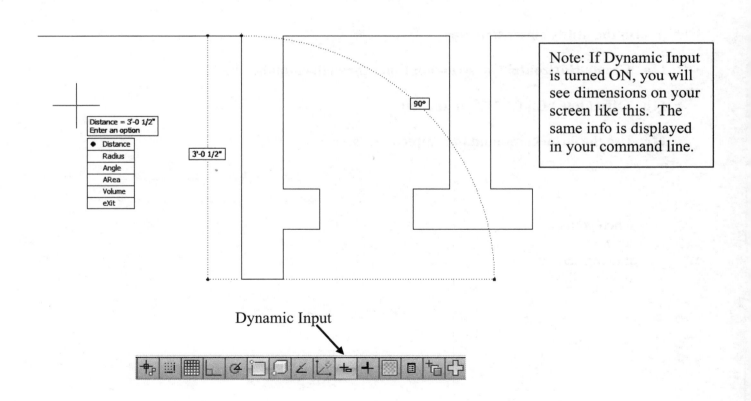

Note: If Dynamic Input is turned ON, you will see dimensions on your screen like this. The same info is displayed in your command line.

Dynamic Input

12b. Press the ↵ Enter key to repeat the Distance command

> *MEASUREGEOM* *Specify first point:* **(Pick an endpoint of line "B")**
> *Specify second point or [Multiple points]:* **(Pick the other endpoint of line "B")**
> *Distance = 2'-0", Angle in XY Plane = 0, Angle from XY Plane = 0*
> *Delta X = 2'-0", Delta Y = 0'-0",   Delta Z = 0'-0"*
> *Enter an option [Distance/Radius/Angle/ARea/Volume/eXit] <Distance>:*

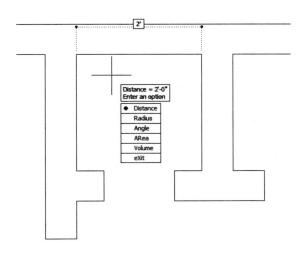

12c. Press the ↵ Enter key to repeat the Distance command

> *MEASUREGEOM* *Specify first point:* **(Pick and endpoint of line "C")**
> *Specify second point or [Multiple points]:* **(Pick the other endpoint of line "C")**
> *Distance = 1'-11", Angle in XY Plane = 90, Angle from XY Plane = 0*
> *Delta X = 0'-0", Delta Y = -1'-11",   Delta Z = 0'-0"*
> *Enter an option [Distance/Radius/Angle/ARea/Volume/eXit] <Distance>: *Cancel**
> **Press the Escape key to end the command**

When you are done, your completed drawing will look like this.

Create the Doors and Windows

The doors for this room are 1-3/4″ thick. There are three doors to the suite. We could create each door individually, but instead, we will take advantage of the Copy, Move, and Mirror commands.

The window glass is 1″ thick, and is centered in the window opening. Let's complete the windows first since that is easier to do.

13. Create the left window

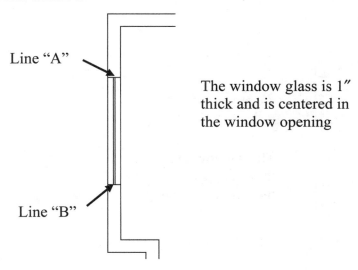

Line "A"

Line "B"

The window glass is 1″ thick and is centered in the window opening

13a. Change the Object Snap setting to ensure Midpoint is selected

13b. Use the Line command to create a line from the Midpoint of line "A" to the Midpoint of line "B"

13c. Offset the line created in step 13b 1/2″ in each direction

The window glass is 1″ thick centered in the opening. Offsetting half the thickness of the glass (in this case it is 1/2″) from the center of the window (which is what we created in step 13b) will give us the full thickness of the glass (1″).

13d. Erase the line created in step 13b

13e. Use the Line command to create 2 vertical lines – one at each endpoint of lines "A" and "B"

When you are done, your drawing should look like this.

14. Create the right window

Line "A"

The window glass is 1″ thick and is centered in the window opening.

Line "B"

Creating this window is identical to creating the left window. Follow the steps used to create the left window to create this window.

15. Create the Entry Door

Hinge point

15a. Draw a 1-3/4″ x 3′ Rectangle starting at the hinge point. Pick the opposite corner to be towards the outside of the room

15b. Create a Horizontal Construction Line from the hinge point

15c. Create a 3′ radius Circle centered on the hinge point

15d. Trim the circle to the construction line and the rectangle

15e. Trim the construction line to the circle and the rectangle

You have now completed the entry door. We will use this same door in the two remaining locations. Notice that the orientation is not identical to the entry door. We will use the Copy, Rotate, Mirror, and Move commands to complete the other doors.

16. Copy the entry door off to the side of your drawing

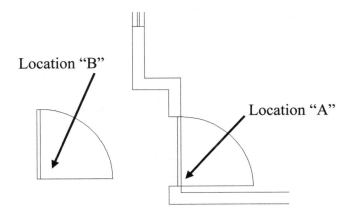

(Pick the Copy command)
COPY Select objects: **(Pick the arc)** *1 found*
Select objects: **(Pick the rectangle)** *1 found, 2 total*
Select objects: **(Pick the line that connects the arc to the rectangle)** *1 found, 3 total*
Select objects: ↵
Current settings: Copy mode = Multiple
Specify base point or [Displacement/mOde] <Displacement>: **(Pick a point near location "A")** *Specify second point or <use first point as displacement>:* **(Pick a point near location "B")**
Specify second point or [Exit/Undo] <Exit>: ↵

17. Create a Mirror image of the copy you just made of the door and swing

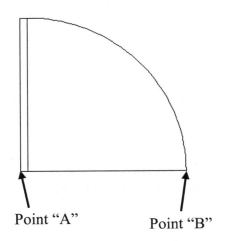

Point "A"   Point "B"

(Pick the Mirror command)
MIRROR *Select objects: (Use a Selection Window to pick the door and swing objects)*
Specify opposite corner: 3 found
Select objects: ↵
Specify first point of mirror line: **(Pick the line near point "A")**
Specify second point of mirror line: **(Pick the line near point "B")**
Erase source objects? [Yes/No] <N>: **y**↵

When you are
done, your
drawing should
look like this.

This door and
swing orientation
can be used for the
bedroom door.

18. Copy the new door and swing from step 17 to the bedroom location

Point "A"

Point "B"

Copy the door from
Point "A" to Point "B"

(Pick the Copy icon)
COPY *Select objects: (Use a Selection Window to pick the door and swing objects)*
Specify opposite corner: 3 found
Select objects: ↵
Current settings: Copy mode = Multiple
Specify base point or [Displacement/mOde] <Displacement>: **(Pick point "A")**
Specify second point or <use first point as displacement>: **(Pick point "B")**
Specify second point or [Exit/Undo] <Exit>: ↵

Because we used the Copy command, we still have the door and swing off to the side of our drawing. We will now change the orientation so that it can be used for the bathroom.

19. Rotate the door and swing to get it in the correct orientation for the bathroom

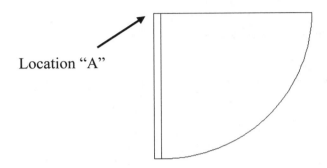

Location "A"

(Pick the Rotate icon)
Current positive angle in UCS: ANGDIR=counterclockwise ANGBASE=0
ROTATE** Select objects: **(Use a Selection Window to pick the door and swing objects)
Specify opposite corner: 3 found
Select objects: ↵
Specify base point: **(Pick a point near location "A")**
Specify rotation angle or [Copy/Reference] <0>: **-90**↵

When you are done, your drawing should look like this.

This door and swing orientation can be used for the bathroom door.

20. Move the door and swing to the bathroom location

Move the door from Point "A" to Point "B"

Point "B"

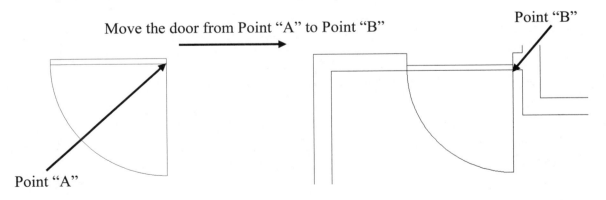

Point "A"

Congratulations! You have now completed the floor plan walls, doors, and windows for the hotel suite.

When you are done, your completed drawing will look like this:

Remember to Save your drawing. We will continue building the Hotel Suite in the next Tutorial.

Chapter 7
Commands – Set 3: Laying-out Your Drawing for Printing

Learning Objectives:

- **Understand the difference between Model Space and Paper Space**
- **Creating Viewports on your Layout to see your Model Space objects**
- **Changing the size and location of the Viewport on your Layout**
- **Setting and Locking the Scale of the Viewport**
- **Setting up and Plotting from Paper Space**
- **Renaming, adding, and deleting Layout tabs**

Model Space & Paper Space

Model Space

All the drawing work we have been doing so far has been in the Model tab and the space we have been drawing in is called Model Space. In Model Space, the designer creates the objects full scale.

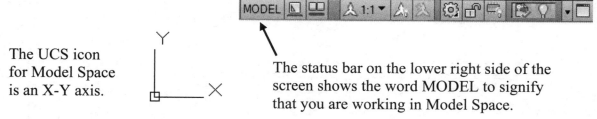

The UCS icon
for Model Space
is an X-Y axis.

The status bar on the lower right side of the screen shows the word MODEL to signify that you are working in Model Space.

Since we need to convey the drawing to the client on a standard format and to scale, such as ¼″ =1′, AutoCAD® allows you to do that using what is known as Paper Space.

On the bottom of the AutoCAD® drawing screen there are several tabs. The left-most tab is the Model tab. This is where we have been creating our objects. The other tabs are the Layout tabs. The Layout tabs are where we use Paper Space to create a finished layout of a drawing for printing.

Paper Space

Paper Space can be accessed only by using a layout tab. You cannot work in Paper Space on the Model tab. Paper Space is used for items such as a drawing border, title block, drawing notes, schedules, and to display different views of the model. Paper Space is scaled 1:1 to the paper you print on. As an example, if you use ¼″ high characters in Paper Space, when you print it out, they will measure ¼″ in height.

The UCS icon
for Paper Space
is a triangle.

The status bar shows the word PAPER to signify that you are working in Paper Space.

Viewports

Viewports are used to view specific areas of the model. You can think of viewports as windows that show different views of the model. Viewports can be different sizes and shapes. The default shape is rectangular. The shape of the viewport on some of the drawing templates is a polygon (AutoCAD® calls this a Polyline).

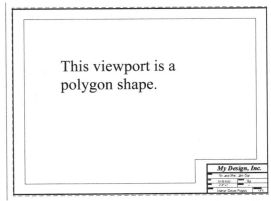

The border that defines the viewport is a Paper Space object, and can be on its own layer, have its own color, and it can be erased, re-sized, or moved just like any rectangle or polygon can.

A Layout can have more than one viewport. As an example of multiple viewports, download the file *Conference Room.dwg* from the publisher website and open the drawing. Pick the Viewport Example tab. It shows two viewports, one showing the chair, and the other showing the plant. The objects were created in Model Space in different locations on the drawing space. The viewports allow you to look at the model objects – which can be positioned in the viewport using Pan and Zoom.

Viewports Tool

The icon is a fly-out style. The last used icon in the list will appear at the top of the list.

The Viewports tool allows you to easily create additional viewports. You can create a single viewport by selecting the Rectangular viewport icon located on the Layout Viewports Panel of the Layout Tab.

Once selected, the command line prompts you with the following:

-VPORTS Specify corner of viewport or
[ON/OFF/Fit/Shadeplot/Lock/Object/Polygonal/Restore/Layer/2/3/4] <Fit>:

For a simple rectangular shaped viewport, simply specify opposite corners on the Paper Space drawing.

As an example, let's start with the single view drawing of the chair. Pick the "Try It" tab to find the following:

To create a second viewport, use the Single Viewport icon, and select two opposite corners to define a second rectangular viewport to the right of the existing viewport:

To make a viewport active, use Ctrl-R to toggle between viewports.

Notice that the new viewport does not show the objects of the model the way that we want it. We can now switch to Model Space by selecting the PAPER button on the status bar, so that it becomes a MODEL button. This will activate the viewport. If the active viewport is not the new viewport, you can use Ctrl-R to toggle the active viewport.

Use the wheel mouse to Pan and Zoom to find the plant. Change the scale by using the scale on the status bar. Select a scale of 1-1/2″ = 1′.

Select the scale using the pull-down arrow of the Viewport Scale icon.

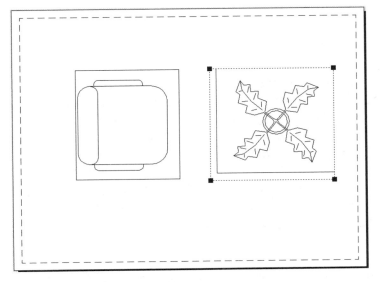

After you get the scale set, you may still have objects in the viewport that are visible that you don't want. You can re-size the viewport to show only the objects you want by using Grips.

Re-Sizing a Viewport

We had discussed Grips (those little blue boxes) in a previous chapter, and we chose to use the Escape key to get rid of them. Re-sizing a Viewport is a situation where Grips come in handy. When you are in Paper Space with no active command in the command line, pick the viewport border. The Grips will appear at each corner of the viewport. You can Pick and drag a Grip and the size of the Viewport will change. It may be best to turn the OSNAP off to do this.

After re-sizing, the extra lines are eliminated from the view of the plant while maintaining the Viewport Scale.

Access Model Space in the Layout tab

Although we have been working on our model using the Model tab, we can also work on our model in the Layout tab, as long as at least one viewport is created. While in the Layout tab, pick the PAPER button on the status bar. The text on the button will become MODEL, the UCS icon will change from a triangle to an X-Y axis, the cursor crosshairs are only visible in the active viewport, and the viewport border will thicken or highlight.

If you have more than one viewport, only one viewport border will thicken/highlight. This signifies that it is the active or current viewport. You can make a different viewport active/current by clicking in it or by holding the Ctrl key and the letter R simultaneously (Ctrl-R). Using Ctrl-R allows you to toggle between viewports.

Once the viewport is active, you can create or modify the Model Space objects, and you can Pan or Zoom to make the objects fit the viewport better.

Create and Modify Objects in a Layout Viewport

Creating or modifying Model Space objects in the Layout tab is best done by using the Maximize Viewport button on the status bar. The maximized layout viewport expands to fill the drawing area. The center point and the layer visibility settings of the viewport are retained, and the surrounding objects are displayed.

↑
Maximize Viewport button

Once you maximize the viewport, the button changes to a Minimize Viewport button, and the toggle arrows are active.

Maximize Previous Viewport ⟶ ⟵ Maximize Next Viewport
toggle arrow   toggle arrow

↑
Minimize Viewport button

You can pan and zoom while you are working in Model Space, but when you restore the viewport (using the Minimize Viewport button) to return to Paper Space, the position and scale of the objects in the layout viewport are restored.

Adjust the View in a Layout Viewport

If you plan to pan the view and change the visibility of layers (Layers will be discuss later), double-click inside a layout viewport to access model space. The viewport border becomes thicker, and the crosshair cursor is visible in the current viewport only. All other viewports in the layout remain visible while you work. You can freeze and thaw layers in the current viewport in the Layer Properties Manager, and you can pan the view. To return to paper space, double-click an empty area on the layout outside a viewport. The changes you made are displayed in the viewport.

If you set the scale in the layout viewport before you access model space, you can lock the scale to prevent changes. When the scale is locked, you cannot use ZOOM while you work in model space.

To accurately and consistently scale each displayed view in the plotted drawing, set the scale of each view relative to paper space. You can change the view scale of the viewport using the Viewport Scale button on the Status bar.

↑
Viewport Scale button

When you work in a layout, the scale factor represents a ratio between the actual size of the model displayed in the viewports and the size of the layout. Changing the scale factor can be done while in Model Space by using the pull-down arrow of the Viewport Scale button. As an example, the Conference Room drawing is scaled at ¼″ =1′. This is a standard scale that was set by using the pull-down arrow on the Viewport Scale button.

Note that scaling or stretching the layout viewport border, while in Paper Space, does not change the scale of the view of the model within the viewport.

Lock the Scale of Layout Viewports

Once you've set the viewport scale, if you zoom in within the viewport, you change the viewport scale at the same time. By locking the viewport scale first, you can zoom in to view different levels of detail in your viewport without altering the viewport scale.

Scale locking will lock the scale that you set for the selected viewport. Once the scale is locked, you can continue to modify the objects in the viewport without affecting the viewport.

To lock the Viewport scale, pick the Lock/Unlock Viewport icon on the status bar:

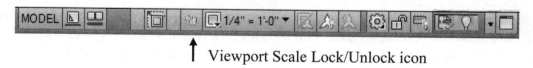

↑ Viewport Scale Lock/Unlock icon

Once selected, the icon now appears as a closed padlock:

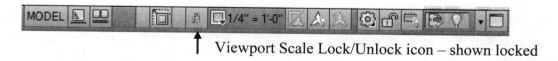

↑ Viewport Scale Lock/Unlock icon – shown locked

The current viewport's scale is locked. If you change the zoom factor in the viewport, only paper space objects are affected.

Plotting from Paper Space

Paper Space was created to allow you to set up your drawing, which was done in real world size, for printing on select size paper. The paper size can be chosen from multiple standard sizes.

Plot, Plot Preview and Page Setup can be found under the Application Menu Browser.

If a printer/plotter is not selected for the layout, selecting Plot Preview from Application Menu Browser will result in the following message above the active command line:

Command: _PREVIEW No plotter is assigned. Use Page Setup to assign a plotter to the current Layout.

Both paper size and assigning a printer/plotter are chosen from the Page Setup Manager.

Page Setup Manager

The Page Setup Manager can be found under the Application Menu Browser and the icon can be found under the Layout Panel of the Layout Tab.

Page Setup icon

When you select Page Setup the Page Setup Manager dialog box appears. Pick the Modify button.

Pick the Modify button to setup the layout for printing/plotting.

The Page Setup dialog box for the current layout will appear.

Select the Printer/plotter here

Select the paper size here

Choose the orientation here

Use the pull-down arrow in the Paper size section of the dialog box to select the size of the paper to print. This will also change the size of the Layout drawing area to match.

This is a partial listing of the sizes available. Only the Inch sizes available are shown.

Use the pull down arrow to select the printer you plan to use.

The choices of printers/ plotters that are available depend on what is loaded on your computer.

For this example, the Adobe PDF is chosen. This will create a Portable Data File (PDF) which can be viewed on any computer that has a PDF reader. If you do not have a PDF reader on your computer, you can download a free version of Adobe Acrobat reader from the Internet at www.adobe.com. Although the reader is free, the writer must be purchased. Other PDF readers and writers are also available.

Once a printer/plotter has been selected, the Preview button is now active. You can preview what the drawing will look like before you print it by selecting the Preview button.

Some printers have a limited print area. Although they can print on standard size paper, the actual area available for printing varies by each printer model. The actual print area will likely be smaller than the entire sheet. Adjustments can be made to your layout border in Paper Space, and additional adjustments can be made by changing the X-Y values in the Plot offset portion of the dialog box.

Additional adjustments can be made to fit your plotter/printer by changing the X-Y values here.

Use the Preview button to ensure satisfactory results before printing on paper.

Once you select the Preview button, a preview of the drawing will appear. To return to the Page Setup dialog box, press the Escape key or the ⏎ Enter key. When you are satisfied with the setup, press the OK button to exit the dialog box. Press the Close button to exit the Page Setup Manager dialog box.

Plotting/Printing Your Drawing

Use the Application Menu Browser to select Print (or Plot under the sub-menu of Print).

A Plot dialog box will appear. Additional plotting changes can be made here prior to printing/ plotting. Many choices are similar to the Plot Manager dialog box.

Pick the OK button to send the drawing to the printer/plotter. A balloon will appear on the lower right side of the screen that indicates that plotting was successful.

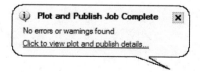

Model & Layout Tabs

Initial AutoCAD® drawings have three tabs displayed at the bottom of the screen as follows:

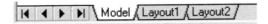

The Model tab is the one that AutoCAD® defaults to. It is for Model Space objects, and is the one that we have been doing all of our drawing work in. The Layout tabs display the Paper Space.

The Layout tabs can be renamed for your convenience. A typical name that you may find would be Sheet 1 or Sheet 2, etc. Or, you could name them Floor Plan, Elevation, etc. It is up to you. The Model tab cannot be renamed.

Renaming Layout Tabs

To rename the Layout tabs, use the following instructions:

Right-click on the tab that you wish to rename. A dialog box of choices appears. Select Rename.

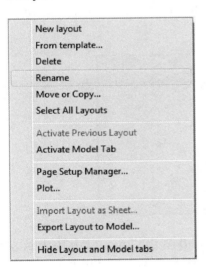

A current layout name highlights and is ready for editing. For this example, let's assume you wish to name this Sheet 1. Type Sheet 1 for the new name.

Notice that the tab has been renamed to the new name that you typed in.

Adding a Layout Tab

Let's assume that you already have Sheet 1 and Sheet 2 for named layout tabs:

If you have a drawing that requires more than two sheets, you may wish to add another tab. To do that, use the following instructions:

Right-click on the Sheet 2 tab to bring up the dialog box. Pick Move or Copy… from the choices you are given.

The Move or Copy dialog box appears. Pick the (move to end) choice and put a check mark in the Create a copy check-box.

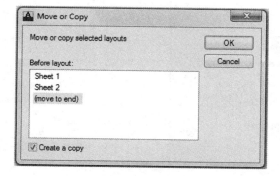

A copy of Sheet 2 is created and added to the end of the layout tab listing. AutoCAD® automatically assigns the name of Sheet 2 (2) for this new layout tab.

Rename this new tab to Sheet 3 using the same technique as describe above for renaming layout tabs.

Add Layout from Template

If you want to use a standard template for your layout, or one that you created, you can add a layout tab that way as well.

Right-Click on a layout tab to bring up the dialog box. Pick From template...

The Select Template From File dialog box appears. Pick the Tutorial-iArch template:

The Insert Layouts dialog will appear. For this template, only one layout style will appear. Pick the OK button.

A new tab is created and the default name is D-Size Layout. This can be renamed.

This layout is an architectural drawing format with the titleblock along the right side and has a single viewport that has a pre-set, locked scale of 1/4″=1′. This can be changed to whatever you desire.

If you want to change anything on this template for future use, you may want to do that starting with a blank drawing and renaming the template.

This template is a 24″ x 36″ size. This would represent a standard size for an architectural firm, but for most people, printing this at home may not be practical. You may be able to find a local print shop that could print your drawing for you on large paper.

Deleting Layout Tabs

To delete a layout tab, use the following instructions:

Right-Click on the Layout tab you wish to delete. A dialog box appears. Pick Delete from your given choices.

A warning dialog box appears. This dialog box warns you that by taking this action, the layout will be permanently deleted. Pick the OK button.

Your selected layout is now deleted and no longer appears as a tab on the lower part of your screen.

Summary

In this chapter you have learned to:

- Understand the concept of Model Space and Paper Space
- Create a viewport using the Viewport toolbar
- Re-size a viewport
- Set and lock the scale of the viewport
- Set up for plotting using Page Setup Manager
- Plot your drawing from Paper Space
- Rename Layout tabs
- Add or delete Layout tabs

Review Questions

1. Why does AutoCAD® have both Model Space and Paper Space?

2. What is the difference between Model Space and Paper Space?

3. What is a Layout?

4. What is an easy way to change the size/shape of a Viewport?

5. What is the advantage of using Paper Space?

6. Does changing the scale of the Viewport change the size of the objects themselves?

7. To print your drawing, what do you need to do first to set it up for printing?

8. The AutoCAD® default template provides two Layout tabs named Layout 1 and Layout 2. How can you add more Layout tabs and rename them?

9. Why can't you delete the Model tab?

10. Why can't you access Paper Space from the Model tab?

Exercises

1. Starting with the Conference Room of Chapter 5 Exercise 1 (or a different drawing you have created already), create a Title Block on Layout 1 Tab in Paper Space. You may need to Zoom and Pan the view of the conference room off to the side to improve your visibility.

While in Model Space, Pan and Zoom your view of the conference room to the side so that you can draw the Title Block with better visibility. After you do this, make sure to switch to Paper Space before drawing the Title Block.

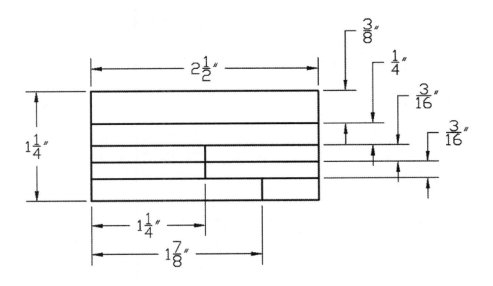

Title Block Dimensions

2. In Paper Space, add to Exercise 1 by drawing a 10-1/2″ x 8″ border. Position the border so that it fits well on the layout. Move the Title Block to the lower right-hand corner. Use Grips to re-size the Viewport so it does not cross the Title Block. Rename the Layout Tab as "Sheet 1".

3. After you complete Exercise 2, switch back to Model Space to set the scale and place the view of the conference room properly on the drawing format. Set and Lock the Viewport Scale to ¼″ = 1′. You may have to re-size the viewport again to make sure the entire conference room is in the viewport.

4. After completing Exercise 3, set up and plot the conference room drawing. Use the Page Setup Manager to select the proper paper size for your printer. Use the Preview button to ensure that your drawing will plot correctly for your printer. Make size adjustments using plot offset and make a print of your drawing.

Chapter 8
Hotel Suite Project – Tutorial 3

Learning Objectives:

- **To continue creating a drawing of a real-world application of AutoCAD®**
  - o **Create a layout for plotting the plan view of the hotel suite at a standard scale**
  - o **Create a drawing border and titleblock for the layout**
  - o **Set up and plot the layout**
  - o **Create a drawing template**
- **To utilize and reinforce the use of the AutoCAD® commands learned in the previous chapters**

This tutorial builds on Tutorial 2 found in Chapter 6. We will use Paper Space for a layout of the model created; set and lock the scale of the drawing; create a drawing border and titleblock; and set up and plot the layout. When you are finished with this tutorial, you will have a scaled printout of the floor plan.

The following commands and techniques will be used:

Commands & Techniques:

- Opening an existing drawing
- Zoom
- Pan
- Toggle Paper/Model Space
- Viewport Scale
- Viewport Lock/Unlock
- Grips - Stretching
- Page Setup Manager
- Printing
- Rectangle
- Move
- Construction Line
- Offset
- Renaming a Layout Tab
- Save
- Save as…

Create a Layout for Plotting

Before beginning, open the Hotel Suite drawing that you updated in Tutorial 2.

1. Use the Layout tab to see how your drawing will look when printed:

Pick the Layout1 tab at the bottom of the drawing screen:

AutoCAD® will bring you to the Paper Space of Layout1.

When in the Paper Space mode of Layout1, your drawing screen will look similar to that shown above. Notice the UCS icon is a triangle shape. This is how it appears when you are in the Paper Space mode.

Depending on where you drew the hotel suite relative to the drawing area, the hotel suite may not appear exactly as shown here.

2. Switch from Paper Space mode to Model Space mode:

(Pick the PAPER toggle) near the bottom of your screen:

Once you pick the toggle, it will switch from Paper Space mode to Model Space mode, and the toggle will display the word MODEL.

In addition, the outline of the Viewport becomes highlighted, and the Model Space UCS icon and the Navigation Cube appear inside the Viewport. This is shown in the following figure.

3. Pan and Zoom the model to fit on the layout:

Using your mouse wheel, relocate and size the model so that it fits on the layout. Note that the default layout size is 8-1/2″ x 11″ for a standard paper printer.

When you print your drawing, you want to be able to print it at a standard scale. When we used the Zoom and Pan commands to change the way the model was displayed on the layout, we did not set it to any specific scale factor. Let's try the scale factor of ¼″ = 1′, which is typical for Interior Design. Sometimes, another standard scale may be required. This would depend on the size of the room, and the size of the paper you want to plot it on.

4. Set and lock the scale of the drawing relative to the paper:

(Pick the Viewport Scale icon) at the bottom right side of the screen. Then select the 1/4″=1′ scale:

Pick ¼″=1′ →

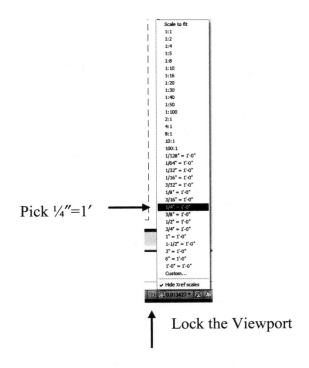

↑ Lock the Viewport

The scale of your drawing should now be ¼"=1′ relative to the paper. You may have noticed a slight change in the size of the drawing on your layout.

(Pick the Lock/Unlock Viewport icon) to lock the display.

Any time that you attempt to zoom when the viewport scale is locked, the following message will appear above the active command line:

Viewport is view-locked. Switching to Paper space.
Switching back to Model space.

(Pick the Model toggle) to switch back to Paper Space.

(Pick the Viewport border) to get Grips. Use the Grips to re-size the Viewport and fit the entire floor plan on the paper.

5. Select the printer and plot:

(Pick the Page Setup icon on the Layout Panel of the Layout Tab)

The Page Setup Manager dialog box will appear.

(Pick the Modify... button)

The Page Setup dialog box will appear.

(Use the pull-down arrow to select the printer)

You must have a printer connected to print. It may have defaulted to "None". Use the pull-down arrow to select a printer.

Once a printer is selected, several items that were grayed-out are now available. In this example, a Canon Inkjet MP 160 Printer was chosen as the printer:

- The pull-down for Paper size is all the available sizes for your chosen printer.
- The Plot scale section will allow you to fit your print to the size of the paper or select a specific scale.
- You can preview your plot by selecting the preview button

If you are satisfied....

(Pick OK to print)

A display showing the progress of your plotting will appear. After it is complete, a notification balloon will appear at the bottom right of your screen.

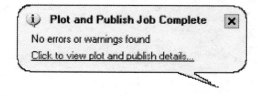

Create a Drawing Format

If you want to make your drawing look even more professional, you can add a Title Block and Border to create a drawing Format. Remember, these are drawn as Paper Space objects.

For the 8-1/2″ x 11″ paper, let's create the same Title Block and Border that was done for one of the Exercises of Chapter 7. The dimensions of the border are 7-3/4″ x 10-1/4″ and the dimensions for the Title Block are shown below:

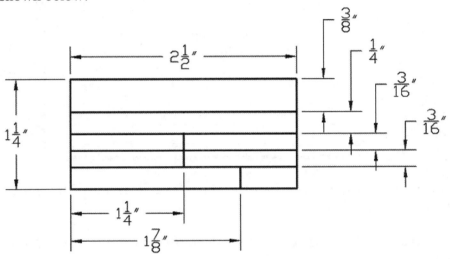

Title Block Dimensions

6. **Create the drawing format in Paper Space.** *(Pick the Model toggle)* **to change to Paper Space.**

6a. **Draw a rectangle 10-1/4″ in the Horizontal direction and 7-3/4″ in the Vertical direction to create the border around the paper**

6b. **Use the Move command to locate the rectangle for best fit on the layout**

6c. **Draw the 2-1/2″ x 1-1/4″ rectangle in the lower right corner of the border**

6d. **Use Grips to adjust the size of the Viewport to clear the Title Block**

6e. **Use Construction Line Offset to offset the top horizontal line of the Title Block 3/8″ down**

6f. **Offset the construction line 1/4″ down**

6g. **Offset the construction line from step 6f 3/16″ down**

6h. Offset the construction line from step 6g 3/16″ down

6i. Trim the construction lines using the rectangle as a cutting edge

Viewport

Title Block rectangle – use as a cutting edge

Trim construction lines to the Title Block rectangle

6j. Use Construction Line Offset to offset the left vertical line of the Title Block 1-1/4″ to the right

6k. Use Construction Line Offset to offset the left vertical line of the Title Block 1-7/8″ to the right

6l. Trim the vertical construction lines as shown in the Title Block dimensions

7. Rename the Layout Tab

Let's re-name our Layout tab from "Layout 1" to "Plan View"

7a. Right-click on the Layout 1 tab and pick Rename from the list of choices

New layout
From template...
Delete
Rename
Move or Copy...
Select All Layouts

Activate Previous Layout
Activate Model Tab

Page Setup Manager...
Plot...

Import Layout as Sheet...
Export Layout to Model...

Hide Layout and Model tabs

7b. Type the words "Plan View" in place of the Layout 1

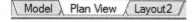

Model   Plan View   Layout2

8. Pick Plot from the File pull-down menu and plot your drawing

Your final plot of the drawing will look like this:

9. Save your drawing.

Create a Template Drawing

Now that we have a drawing with architectural units, and a drawing format with title block, we can save this as a template for future use. We will need to erase all the objects in Model Space so we can have a blank drawing.

10. Create the template drawing.

    10a. Pick the Model tab.

    10b. Zoom to "All" to be able to capture everything on the Model Space.

    10c. Using either a Crossing Window or a Selection Window, erase all the objects in the Model Space.

    10d. Pick File, Save As…, to save the drawing as a template. Under "File of type", pick AutoCAD Drawing Template (*.dwt). AutoCAD® will automatically choose the Template folder as the "Save in" location. Name your template "Interior Design". Pick Save.

10e. A template Options dialog box will appear. If you desire, you may type in a description here. Otherwise, pick OK to close it out.

Now that you have saved this as a drawing template, you can use this when starting a new drawing. We can customize this template further as we desire.

Congratulations! You have now completed Tutorial 3.

Chapter 9
Commands – Set 4: Re-Using Objects and Getting Organized

Learning Objectives:

- **Creating and Using Blocks**
- **Using Design Center to bring Blocks in from other drawings**
- **Creating and using Layers**
- **Changing Properties**
- **Setting Color, Line Type, and Lineweights**

Everything we have done so far, we have had to create ourselves. A big advantage of using AutoCAD® is that you only have to create something once. You can then use what you created multiple times throughout your drawing, and for other drawings as well. In fact, you can use groups of objects (Blocks) that someone else created, which can save you time. In this chapter we will see the major advantage that this has over drawing by hand.

Blocks – Treating Multiple Objects as One

AutoCAD® allows you to group objects together and treat them as one object. The name of this grouping is a Block. This is very useful for many Interior Design objects, such as furniture, fixtures, doors, windows, etc.

Making Blocks

The Create Block command allows you to associate multiple objects so that they are treated as a single object. The icon is on the Block Panel of the Home Tab and also on the Block Definition Panel of the Insert Tab. On the Block Definition Panel, the icon is a fly-out type of icon, with Create Block as the default icon on top. If you use the fly-out to select Write Block, that icon would then appear on top.

Procedure:

Pick (left click): **Create Block icon** from the Block Panel of the Home Tab.
 (As an alternative, use the Block Definition Panel of the Insert Tab)

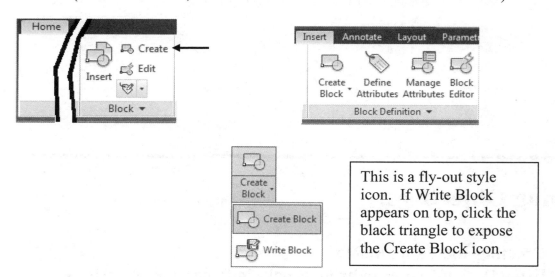

This is a fly-out style icon. If Write Block appears on top, click the black triangle to expose the Create Block icon.

The Block Definition dialog box will appear. This is where you specify the name of your block, the objects that make it up, and the insertion base point:

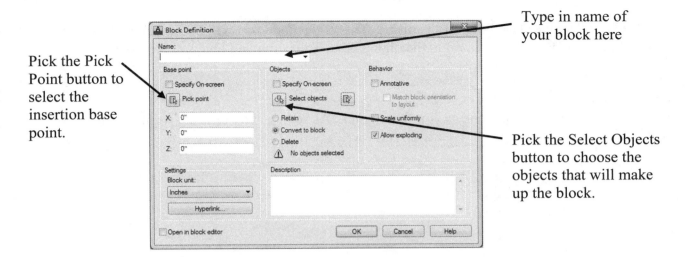

Type in name of
your block here

Pick the Pick
Point button to
select the
insertion base
point.

Pick the Select Objects
button to choose the
objects that will make
up the block.

As an example, download the file *Telephone.dwg* from the publisher's website, open the drawing, and select the Create Block icon. This is an example of multiple objects that should be treated as a single item on your drawing.

We will type in the name "Telephone" for the name of the block.

We need to select the objects that make up the block. Pick the Select Objects button in the dialog box. The dialog box will disappear and the command line will prompt you to select the objects. Use a Selection Window to select all the objects that make up the telephone.

BLOCK *Select objects:*
Select objects: Specify opposite corner: 747 found
Select objects: ↵

Once all the objects are selected, press the ↵ Enter key.

The dialog box will reappear on your screen. A small image of the objects selected will appear in the dialog box.

We need to select the Base Point of the block. This is the point that will become the origin of the block. Select the Pick point button in the dialog box. The command line will prompt you to select the insertion base point.

Specify insertion base point:
Pick any object on the telephone as your base point. As soon as you pick the point, the dialog box will reappear.

Pick the OK button to exit the dialog box, and the Block command will exit automatically.

You have now created a block of the telephone. Since we left the radio button selected to "Convert to block", the existing objects that make up the telephone are now joined as a block. You can confirm this with the List command.

LIST *Select objects: 1 found*

Select objects: ↵

> BLOCK REFERENCE *Layer: "0"*
>   *Space: Model space*
>   *Handle = a78*
> *Block Name: "Telephone"*
>   *at point, X=1'-2 3/8" Y=0'-9 15/16" Z=0'-0"*
> *X scale factor: 1.0000*
> *Y scale factor: 1.0000*
> *rotation angle: 0*
> *Z scale factor: 1.0000*
>   *InsUnits: Inches*
> *Unit conversion: 1.0000*
> *Scale uniformly: Yes*
> *Allow exploding: Yes*

Your X and Y values may be different than shown here; it is dependent on where you selected your Pick Point.

Also, your Handle name may be different than shown. The Handle name is how AutoCAD® tracks each object – nothing for us to worry about.

Inserting Blocks

The Insert Block command allows you to insert Blocks into your drawing. These can be blocks that were created within the drawing, or the complete insertion of an external drawing. The icon is on the Block Panel of the Insert Tab.

Procedure:

Pick (left click): **Insert Block icon** from the Block Panel of the Home Tab.
  (As an alternative use the Block Panel of the Insert Tab)

The Insert dialog box will appear. This is where you select the block to insert into your drawing.

To Pick a location on the drawing to insert your block, make sure the check-box Specify On-screen is checked.

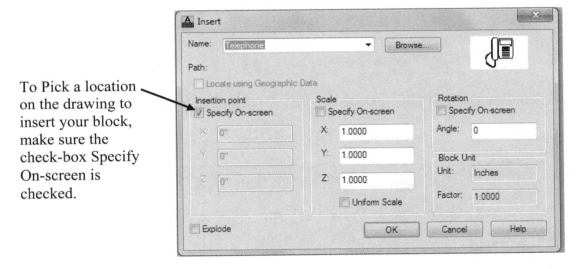

Use the pull-down arrow to select from the list of blocks that are currently in the drawing. In this example, the Telephone is the only block available.

Once you have selected the block you want to insert, you need to determine where to place it on your drawing. Under the Insertion point section of the dialog box, make sure there is a check mark in the check box for Specify On-screen. This allows you to pick a point on the drawing to place the block. Pick the OK button. The dialog box will disappear, an image of your block will follow your cursor, and the command line will prompt you to specify the location for the block:

INSERT Specify insertion point or [Basepoint/Scale/X/Y/Z/Rotate]: **Pick a location on your screen to insert the block.**

The block will appear on your drawing and the command will end.

If you select the Browse button, the Select Drawing File dialog box will appear. This is very similar to an Open File dialog box. Using the Browse button method will insert an entire drawing into your current drawing. It will not limit it to just a specific Block from that drawing. You can try this on your own.

In order to select a specific Block from a drawing other than the current drawing, AutoCAD® has the Design Center feature.

Design Center

The Design Center feature of AutoCAD® allows you to use items that were created on other drawings, and bring them into your current drawings. It is especially useful for Blocks, but can also be used for other things such as Dimension Styles, Layers, Text Styles, Layouts, etc.

You can bring up the Design Center palette by selecting the Design Center icon, located on the Content Panel of the Insert Tab.

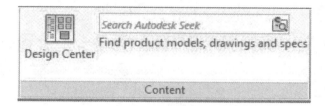

Once you select the icon, the Design Center palette will appear on your screen:

The appearance of the Design Center palette is very similar to the Windows tool My Computer. The left side of the palette shows a Tree View or hierarchy of folders that are on your computer. The right side of the palette shows the contents of the selected folder or file. If the Tree View is not displayed, pick the Tree View Toggle at the top of the palette to bring it up.

When you initially bring up the Design Center, AutoCAD® may open the folder within the AutoCAD® program to the samples that were provided with the program. Use the Tree on the left side to select the folder you want. Using the Views selector icon can control the method by which the contents are displayed. In this example, the display is using Large icons.

> If you always want the Design Center to open a specific folder when you first bring it up, you can right-click on that folder and select "Set as Home" from the shortcut menu. In addition, if there are multiple folders that you want to access frequently, you can right click on each folder (one at a time) and select "Add to Favorites" from the shortcut menu.

Using Design Center

The following examples assume that you currently have a drawing open and you wish to bring in items from existing drawings. It also assumes that you have already opened the Design Center palette and selected the drawing of your choice.

Bring Blocks into Your Drawing:

Blocks that were previously created, other than those in the drawing you are currently working on, are easy to bring into your drawing by using the Design Center.

1. Double-click the Blocks icon on the right side of the Design Center palette. The alternative is to expand the drawing by picking on the "+" in front of that drawing on the left side of the Design Center palette and then single-click the Blocks icon.
2. The right side of the Design Center palette now displays all the blocks contained in the drawing. Click on the block of your choice and drag it into your drawing. An alternate method is to double-click on the block of your choice and follow the instructions of the Insert dialog box that appears.

Double-clicking the block will bring up the Insert dialog box.

Bring Styles, etc. into Your Drawing

Bringing other items, such as Dimension Styles, Text Styles, Layers, Layouts, etc. are done in the same manner as bringing Blocks into your drawing. The only difference is that it may not be as obvious that it was brought into the drawing. You can use the Styles toolbar to verify that the Dimension Styles, Text Styles, and Table Styles were brought in. Use the Layers Manager to verify that Layers were brought in, etc.

Layers

Layers are available in AutoCAD®. Layers can be thought of as see-through sheets that are stacked on top of each other. You can use layers to organize and manage your objects. You can make specific layers invisible by turning them off or freezing them. You can lock any layer so that any objects on that layer cannot be changed. Some design teams require you to follow specific naming conventions for your layers, and other teams do not. If you are working independently, as the designer, it is your choice how you use and name layers. You can add any number of layers. Once layers are created, and you no longer need them, they can also be deleted. You cannot delete Layer 0. It is the default layer for AutoCAD® drawings. If you bring items in using Design Center, AutoCAD® will create a layer named Defpoints. You cannot delete this layer either – just ignore it.

The Layers Panel is on the Home Tab:

Layer Properties Manager icon

Pull-down arrow allows you to view all layers available

Displays Current Layer and status

Layer Properties Manager

When you select the Layer Properties Manager icon, a dialog box will appear:

Notice that the dialog box has two sides: the Layer Filter and the Layer Properties. We will not be using Filters, so, these instructions will be limited to Layer Properties.

The dialog box shown has Layer 0. We will use this dialog box to create new layers, and define properties for those layers. When done, pick the "X" to close the dialog box.

Creating a New Layer

Pick the New Layer icon. A new row appears on the list. This represents the new layer and is automatically given a default name of Layer1, which is highlighted and ready for editing. As an example, let's name this layer Existing Structure. Simply type that in place of Layer1.

There are several columns in the Layer Properties display. The width of the columns can be adjusted by moving your cursor to the line separating the column names and dragging. Double-clicking will adjust the column to minimum width and still allow the word to fit.

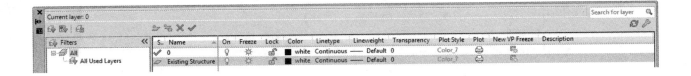

Visibility of Layers

Layers can be turned on or off, frozen or thawed, and locked or unlocked, by picking the relative icon in each column. These icons change as each option is selected:

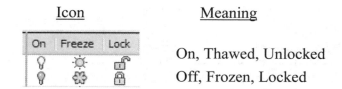

Icon	Meaning
	On, Thawed, Unlocked
	Off, Frozen, Locked

When a layer is turned off or frozen, the objects on that layer become invisible. The difference between the two is subtle – the drawing is regenerated when you thaw a frozen layer, but it is not when you turn a layer that was off back on. The typical designer doesn't care about this subtlety. These differences are not important.

What is important is this: when in a Layout, freezing a layer in the "current viewport" is the best way to control visibility – especially for printing. If you turn a layer off, it is invisible in all viewports; this is usually not what is desired. This difference comes in handy when you have multiple viewports or multiple Layouts.

When a layer is Locked, it remains visible, but you cannot change or delete any of the objects that reside on that layer. This is a good tool for preserving objects, such as those on layers provided by the architect. You use this feature when you don't want to risk changing objects that were provided by others on your design team.

For the new layer we just created, we will leave the icons On, Thawed, and Unlocked.

Assigning a Color to the Layer

To change the color of a layer, pick the color icon in the Color column. When you pick it, the Select Color dialog box will appear.

There are three tabs to choose your color: Index Color, True Color, and Color Books. The index color is shown above and has pre-defined standard colors and numbered colors. The other tabs are illustrated below:

Under the Color Books tab, there is a pull-down arrow that you can use to select from a variety of available color books, including Pantone colors.

Choose the color you desire for your layer then pick the OK button to exit the dialog box.

Assigning a Linetype to the Layer

To change the linetype of a layer, pick the word in the Linetype column (in this case the word is Continuous). When you pick it, the Select Linetype dialog box will appear.

There are a number of different line types to choose from in AutoCAD®, however, they may not be loaded in your drawing yet. These are stored in a common AutoCAD® program file in order to minimize the amount of memory each drawing will require.

As an example, suppose we wish to change the Linetype to a hidden line. Since that is not available in the Select Linetype dialog box, we will have to load it. Pick the Load… button. The Load or Reload Linetypes dialog box will appear.

Scroll down the list to find the Linetype you desire.

Scroll down the list until you find Hidden. Pick on the word Hidden and that Linetype will be highlighted. Then pick the OK button to exit the dialog box and return to Select Linetype dialog box. In that dialog box, the Hidden Linetype is now available as a Linetype choice.

Pick the HIDDEN Linetype to select it, and then pick the OK button to exit the dialog box and return to the Layer Properties Manager dialog box.

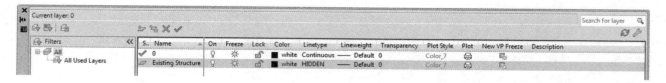

Linetype Scale

Each linetype is defined as a specific size. For a hidden line, AutoCAD defines the length of the dash, and the length of the space between dashes. With large drawings used in interior design, the hidden line may actually appear as a solid line. To correct the visibility of the hidden line, you can change the linetype scale. To change the scale of all linetypes in your drawing, you need to type in the command "ltscale" on the command line:

Example:

Shown here is a countertop with three cabinets underneath. The lines of the cabinets should be dashed because they are hidden lines. We can create those lines on a layer with the linetype of hidden. However, because of the size of the object, it is difficult to distinguish that these are dashed lines.

We can correct this by typing the LTSCALE command. The value of the scale factor can be determined by trial and error.

ltscale↵
LTSCALE *Enter new linetype scale factor <1.0000>:* **10**↵
Regenerating model.

The following shows the results of using the scale factor of 10:

As you can see, the appearance of the hidden lines is much better.

Using the LTSCALE command globally changes the scale factor of all linetypes on your drawing. This may not always be desirable. If you also have centerlines on your drawing, applying the same scale factor may not be desired. In that case, you can use the Properties palette to change the linetype scale of an individual object selected

Current Layer

The Current Layer is the layer that objects will reside on as you draw. There are a number of ways to make a layer the Current Layer. While still in the Layer Properties Manager, you can highlight the layer and pick the Set Current icon. When a layer is the current layer, the green check mark is shown in the Status column for that layer.

Picking the X on the upper left corner of the dialog box will exit the Layer Properties Manager dialog box and return you to the drawing screen.

The Layers Panel on the Home Tab will now show the layer you selected as the Current Layer.

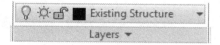

Using the Layers toolbar, you can change the Current Layer by using the pull-down arrow and picking the layer. As an example, let's make layer 0 the Current Layer:

 ← Use your cursor to pick layer 0

Layer 0 is now displayed as the Current Layer:

You can also use the Make Objects Layer Current icon. With nothing in the command line, select an object. The blue grips will display, and the Layers toolbar will show the name of the layer that the object is on.

As an example, suppose there are two circles on the drawing. One circle is on layer 0, and the other is on layer Existing Structure. Regardless of the current layer displayed, when an object is selected, the name of the layer that it resides on will be displayed in the Layer toolbar:

Make Object's
Layer Current icon

Picking the Make Object's Layer Current icon makes the Layer that the selected object is on the Current Layer.

Properties

The Properties Panel is on the Home Tab.

Color Control ⟶

Lineweight Control ⟶

Linetype Control ⟶

Picking this downward arrow accesses the Properties Palette.

All three controls have ByLayer and ByBlock as selection options. The default is ByLayer, which means that the values that were set for that Layer will be used for the objects drawn. ByBlock allows you to retain the properties of the Blocks inserted. You can use these controls to change the properties of individual objects instead of having the entire layer with the object properties. Simply select the object, and then use the pull-down arrow to change to the desired property.

Changing Object Properties

You can change properties of objects using the Properties Palette. The Properties Palette is accessed by picking the downward arrow on the lower right of the Properties Panel. When you select this, the Properties palette will appear:

Object Selection Display ⟶

Using the Properties dialog box allows you to change properties for selected objects. You can change any of the items that are shown in the dialog box. For example, if you want to change the color of an item, pick on Color, and the entire section is highlighted and a pull-down arrow appears. Use the pull-down arrow to select the color. When you are done, close the dialog box by selecting the X in the gray bar of the dialog box. Use the escape key to remove the grips from the selected objects.

<u>Example:</u>

Suppose we had a circle located on the center of the countertop of the previous example, with lines drawn and the linetypes of the lines are set to "center". With the current LTSCALE factor of 10, the centerlines of the circle will appear as follows:

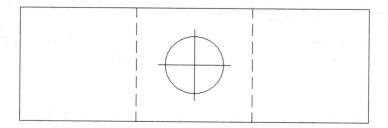

As you can see, they do not properly appear as centerlines. Since we like the scale factor we have chosen for the hidden lines, we do not want to globally change that factor by using the LTSCALE command. Instead, we can use the Properties palette, select the centerlines, and change the Lintype scale factor for those lines.

Here we can see that the two centerlines were selected and the Properties palette Linetype scale portion was also selected. We can simply type in a new scale factor for the centerlines. In this case, a scale factor of .5 seems to work best. Choosing .5 would have been the same as a global scale factor of 5 since a global scale factor of 10 is already applied (.5 x 10 = 5).

After you apply the scale factor to the centerlines, the drawing will look like this:

Lineweight

Typically, the object lines for your designs should be thicker than the dimension lines. That makes it easier to distinguish the items of interest. AutoCAD® has a feature that allows you to control and view the lineweight. This can be done for individual objects or for any object drawn on a layer that has the lineweight defined. This is very similar to assigning colors or linetype.

Before setting the lineweight, make sure the units that you select for lineweight is Inches and not Millimeters. To ensure that you have the correct units, use the pull down arrow of the Lineweight section of the Properties Panel of the Home Tab and pick Lineweight Settings…

The Lineweight Settings dialog box will appear. Ensure that the radio button in front of Inches is selected and the check box for Display Lineweight is checked. When you are done, pick the OK button to close the dialog box.

To change the lineweight of all objects on a specific layer, use the Layer Properties icon to bring up the Layer Properties Manager dialog box.

In this example, we will change the Lineweight of layer Walls to a thicker value than the default value. The default value of Lineweight is set at .25 mm (which is approximately .010 inches). We will choose .020″ to make the lines twice as thick.

In the dialog box, pick on the word Default under the Lineweight column of the layer Walls. A Lineweight dialog box will appear. Scroll down the list of available Lineweights and pick .020″. When you are done, pick the OK button to close the dialog box.

Notice that the new value of the Lineweight for the layer Walls is displayed in the Layer Properties Manager dialog box. Pick the X in the upper left corner to close the dialog box.

The visibility of the thicker lines will not appear on the screen unless you toggle the Show/Hide Lineweight switch on the status bar (or use the check box in the Lineweight Settings dialog box).

Show/Hide Lineweight
Toggle Switch

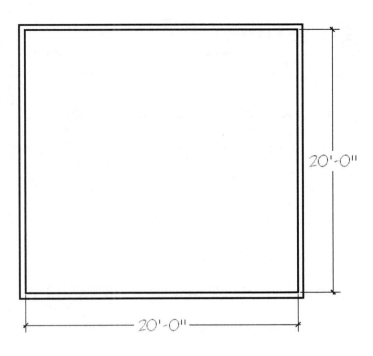

This is an example of the visibility of the lineweights. The object lines are twice as thick as the dimension lines.

Summary

In this chapter you have learned to:

- Group objects together to become a block
- Insert blocks that exist within the drawing or entire files from outside the drawing
- Use Design Center to bring blocks in from other drawings
- Create new layers
- Load new linetypes
- Rename and define properties – color, linetype, lineweight – for layers
- Change properties of individual objects

Review Questions

1. What is a grouping of objects called in AutoCAD®?

2. What method is used to bring Blocks in from other drawings?

3. What other things besides Blocks can be brought into your drawing using Design Center?

4. What is the AutoCAD® name for a solid line type?

5. How do you change a line from solid to hidden?

6. What are Layers and how are they used?

7. How do you change an object line thickness and display it on your screen?

8. What are object properties and how are they changed?

9. How do you correct the visibility of a hidden line if it still appears solid?

10. Why is freezing a layer in the "current viewport" more useful than turning a layer off?

Exercises

1. Open the Conference Room from Exercise 1 of Chapter 5. Use the Insert Block command to import the Conference Chair you created from Exercise 3 of Chapter 5. Use the Copy and Move commands to locate the chairs in the Conference Room.

2. Download the Plant and Conference Phone drawings from the publisher's web site. Use Design Center to put two plants and the conference phone into the Conference Room drawing as shown:

3. Continuing building on Exercise 2 by creating layers "Furniture", "Misc" and "Structure". Assign properties to those layers as shown. After the layers are created, change the layer that the walls and doors from "0" to "Structure"; tables and chairs from "0" to "Furniture"; and the plants and conference phone from "0" to "Misc".

Name	Color	Lineweight
Furniture	magenta	0.012"
Misc	green	Default
Structure	blue	0.012"

4. Draw the Galley Kitchen. Use Design Center to insert the Range, Refrigerator, and Sink. These are provided with the AutoCAD® program, and are also available on the publisher's web site. Create layers "Walls", "Appliances", "Plumbing", and "Cabinets". Place the objects on their corresponding layer.

Notes:

Chapter 10
Hotel Suite Project – Tutorial 4

Learning Objectives:

- **To continue creating a drawing of a real-world application of AutoCAD®**
  - o **Use Design Center to insert furniture Blocks into the plan view**
  - o **Create and use Layers**
  - o **Change object Properties**
- **To utilize and reinforce the use of the AutoCAD® commands learned in the previous chapters**
- **Update the Template drawing**

This tutorial builds on Tutorial 3 found in Chapter 8. In this tutorial, we will put the furniture into our floor plan of the Hotel Suite. In addition, we will create and use layers. We will start with the simple rectangular shapes first. Rather than bring these in as Blocks, we will create them. When you are finished with this tutorial, all the furniture in the plan view of the hotel suite will be completed.

In addition, we will update our template drawing to include layers and lineweights.

Commands & Techniques:

- Opening an existing drawing
- Zoom
- Pan
- Offset
- Fillet
- Trim
- Rectangle
- Copy
- Line
- Move
- Erase
- Design Center
- Rotate
- Explode
- Move
- Layers
- Properties
- Save

Placing Furniture/Fixtures on the Floor Plan

Before beginning, open the Hotel Suite drawing that you updated in Tutorial 3.

Many of the items of furniture, fixtures, etc. are already pre-drawn and have been provided for you in the form of Blocks. However, for the simple items that are rectangular shaped, we will draw those ourselves. The following drawing shows all the rectangular shapes we will draw.

Let's start with the Living Room area and Bathroom. Although a drawing is provided, a listing of items and their sizes are as follows:

End Table:	2′ x 2′
Coffee Table:	3′6″ x 1′10″
Countertop:	5′11″ x 2′1″
Desk:	4′6″ x 2′ 8″
Dresser:	3′10-1/2″ x 1′10″
Vanity:	2′ x wall-to-wall

The vanity in the bathroom is the full length between the walls. The countertop is nestled in the corner of the living room. Both of these pieces are permanently located in place. Since furniture is movable, all pieces are located approximately as shown.

1. **Offset the left bathroom wall 2′ to create the vanity.**

2. **Offset the upper right living room wall lines 5′11″ to the left and 2′1″ down.**

3. **Use either the Fillet or Trim command to complete the countertop.**

4. **Use the Rectangle command to create the End Table, Coffee Table, Desk, and Dresser.**

   - Use the dimensions and drawing to create and locate these items on the plan view.

Now we will create the rectangular shapes in the Bedroom. Although a drawing is provided, a listing of items and their sizes are as follows:

Night Stand: 1′10″ x 1′6″
Desk: 3′ x 1′10″
Dresser: 3′10-1/2″ x 1′10″ (Same as the one in the living room)
Utility Enclosure: 1′3-1/2″ x 3/4″

5. Use the Rectangle command to create the Desk and one Night Stand.

- Use the dimensions and drawing to create and locate these items on the plan view.

6. Use the Copy command to create a second Night Stand.

7. **Use the Copy command to duplicate the dresser created for the living room and locate in the bedroom to the approximate location shown.**

The Utility Closet Enclosure is centered in the opening. In order to get the enclosure located where we want it, we will first create it in the middle of the room, then move it to the center of the opening. To find the center of the opening, we will draw a line across the opening.

8. **Use the Rectangle command to draw the Utility Closet Enclosure in the middle of the bedroom.**

9. **Use the Line command to draw a line across the opening of the utility closet between points "A" & "B".**

Point "A"

Utility Closet

Point "B"

Adding a line between points "A" & "B" will allow us to move the enclosure to the center of this line, which is the center of the opening. We will erase this line after we move the enclosure.

We will now relocate the Utility Closet Enclosure (the rectangle created in step 8) to the center of the opening. We will use Snap to Midpoint to find the middle of the top line of the rectangle, and the middle of the line created in step 9. Prior to moving on to step 10, make sure Object Snap (OSNAP) is turned on and Midpoint is selected. As an alternative, you can use the Snap to Midpoint icon of the Object Snap toolbar twice during the Move command.

10. **Use the Move command to relocate the rectangle created in step 8 to the center of the line created in step 9.**

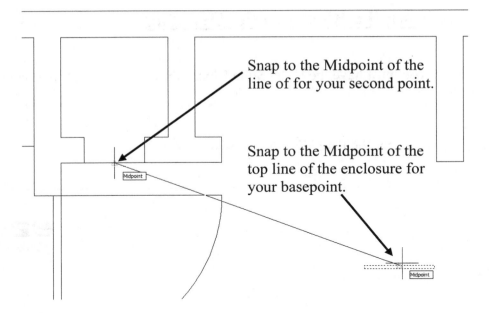

Snap to the Midpoint of the line of for your second point.

Snap to the Midpoint of the top line of the enclosure for your basepoint.

11. Erase the line that was created in step 9. Use a Selection Window (Left-to-Right) to pick just the line and not the rectangle.

When you are done, your completed drawing will look like this:

Now that we have all the rectangular shapes created, we will use Design Center to bring in the blocks for the furniture, fixtures, etc.

Adding the Blocks to the Drawing

Prior to bringing the blocks in, you must have the Hotel Suite Blocks drawing that you can download from the publishers web site.

The Blocks that we are going to use for the Plan View are shown below:

Adding Blocks to the Bedroom

12. Use Design Center to bring in the Blocks for the Bedroom.

(Pick the Design Center icon)

The Design Center Palette will appear on your screen. Using the Tree View on the left side of the Design Center Palette, find the Hotel Suite Blocks drawing.

Once you select the Hotel Suite Block drawing, the right side of the Design Center Palette will look like this:

(Double-click the Blocks icon in the Design Center Palette)

The right side of the palette will now show the small icons representing the blocks.

Let's move the bed into the drawing:

(Pick & Drag the icon of the King Bed with Pillows into the Bedroom)

Pick the icon of the Bed and drag it into a clear area of your drawing.

Once you pick an icon, a thumbnail view will appear in this section of the palette.

(Pick the X in the upper corner of the palette to close it)

We will now locate the bed to the correct location in the room using the Move command. We want the bed to be located so that it is centered and against the wall. This will be easy to do since we can use Snap to Midpoint just like we did for the Utility Closet Enclosure.

13. Use the Move command and move the block of the bed.

Remember, because the bed is a block, it is treated as a single object. However, we can still use Snap to Midpoint of the lower horizontal line of the bed as the basepoint. We will then use the midpoint of the lower wall line for the second point.

14. Continue using the Design Center to bring in additional blocks to complete the bedroom.

- You can bring the blocks in to the side of the Hotel Suite, then use the Move command to locate them in the room. Use the same technique used to locate the Utility Closet Enclosure for the Closet Doors, Closet Rack, and the Curtains.

15. Use the Rotate command to rotate the Luggage Rack 45°.

16. Move the Desk Chair under the desk. Explode the Desk Chair and use the Trim and Erase commands to show that the chair is under the desk.

17. Use the Line command to draw lines corner-to-corner inside the Utility Closet.

When you are done, your drawing will look like this:

Adding Blocks to the Bathroom

18. **Use Design Center to bring in the Blocks for the Bathroom.**

19. **Use the Move command to move the Tub to the lower right hand corner.**

20. **Offset the right wall 1′3-1/4″ to the left.**

21. **Use the Move command to move the Shower Head into position.**

Use the Endpoint of the Offset line created in step 20 as the second point.

Use the Midpoint of the top horizontal line of the Shower Head as the basepoint.

22. Erase the Offset line that was created in step 20.

23. Offset the right wall 4'5-3/4" to the left.

24. Use the Move command to move the Toilet into position.

Use the Endpoint of the Offset line created in step 23 as the second point.

Use the Midpoint of the bottom horizontal line of the Toilet as the basepoint.

25. Erase the Offset line that was created in step 23.

26. Offset the left wall 1' to the right and the lower wall 3'6" up.

27. Use the Move command to move the Sink into position.

Use the Center of the Sink as the basepoint.

Use the Intersection of the offset lines created in step 26 as the second point.

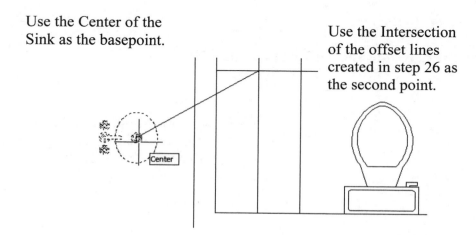

28. Erase the Offset lines that were created in step 26.

When you are done, your drawing will look like this:

Adding Blocks to the Living Room

29. Use Design Center to bring in the Blocks for the Living Room.

We need to locate the Bar Sink on the countertop. The Bar Sink is located as shown:

30. Offset the upper right wall line 1'3" to the left and the upper wall line 1' down.

31. Use the Move command to move the Bar Sink into position.

Use the Center of the Bar Sink as the basepoint.

Use the Intersection of the offset lines created in step 30 as the second point.

32. Erase the Offset lines that were created in step 30.

33. Use the Copy command to create 2 more Desk Chairs.

34. Continue to use the Move command to locate all the other items in the Living Room except for the Curtain.

35. Use the Rotate command to rotate the Flat Screen TV, one of the Desk Chairs, and the Curtains 180°. Rotate the Telephone -90°.

- Note that the Curtains should still be off to the side of your drawing.

36. Use the Move command to move the Curtains into position.

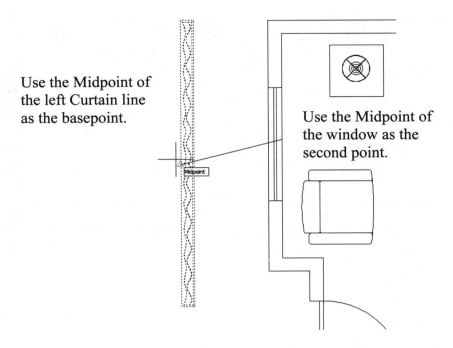

Use the Midpoint of
the left Curtain line
as the basepoint.

Use the Midpoint of
the window as the
second point.

37. Explode the Curtain block and use the Trim and Erase commands to complete the Living Room window treatment.

You are now done inserting all the Blocks onto the Plan View. Save your drawing.

When you are done, your drawing will look like this:

Creating Layers

Now that we have the Floor Plan completed, we can create layers and move the objects to the new layers. This will allow us to show only the items that we want to see. For this tutorial, we will create layers "Structure", "Furniture", "Fixtures", and "Misc". We will assign colors and lineweights to each layer.

38. Bring up the Layer Properties Manager. The icon is on the Layers Panel of the Home Tab.

Layer Properties
Manager icon

(Pick Layer Properties Manager icon)

The Layer Properties Manager dialog box will appear.

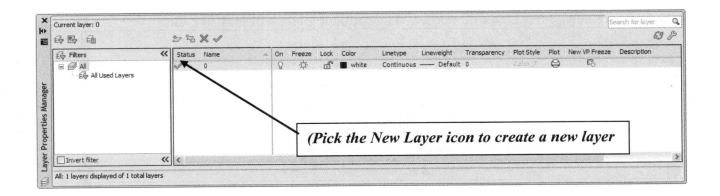

39. Add new layers and name them as shown:

40. Using the Standard colors, change the color of layer "Structure" to green; layer "Furniture" to blue; layer "Fixtures" to magenta, layer "Misc" to red, and layer Viewport to cyan. Layer "Format" will remain white. In addition, change the Lineweight of layer "Format" to .020; layer "Structure" to .012"; layers "Furniture", "Fixtures", and "Misc" to .010".

Standard
Colors

When you are done, your Layer Properties Manager dialog box will look like this:

(Pick the "X" in the upper LH corner of the dialog box to close it)

41. Use the Properties palette to change the layer for the walls, doors, and windows.

(Pick the downward arrow on the Properties Panel of the Home Tab to access the Properties Palette)

The Properties palette will appear:

(Pick all the objects that make up the walls, doors, and windows)

It is not necessary to select all the objects at once – you can repeat the process until all objects that belong on this layer have been changed. You can pick anywhere in the drawing space and press the Esc key to eliminate the selection set. This is helpful if you do not pick all the items at once.

After you begin to select the objects do the following:

(Pick Layer and use the pull-down arrow to select layer "Structure")

Pick Layer

Use the pull-down arrow to select layer "Structure".

42. Close the Properties Palette and press the Esc key.

When you are done, your drawing will look like this:

43. Use the pull-down arrow in the Layers toolbar to turn layer "Structure" off.

After turning the light bulb off, pick anywhere in the drawing space to close out this pull-down.

With layer "Structure" turned off, it is easier to select the other objects to change their layer.

44. Repeat the process described in steps 41 & 42 to change the layer for the furniture, fixtures, and miscellaneous items.

You can turn layers on and off as desired to help facilitate selecting the objects.

When you are done, your drawing will look like this:

45. Pick the Plan View tab and switch to Paper Space

46. Use a Selection Window or a Crossing Window to select the drawing format with the titleblock. The grips will appear. Use the pull-down arrow on the Layers toolbar and pick layer Format. This changes all the selected objects to layer Format. Use the Escape key to eliminate the grips.

47. Pick the viewport border. Use the pull-down arrow on the Layers toolbar and pick layer Viewport. This changes the viewport border to layer Viewport. Use the Escape key to eliminate the grips.

Congratulations! Save your drawing – we will continue to build on this in the next tutorial.

Add Layers to Template

Let's take advantage of the layers we created in this tutorial and build them into our drawing template.

48. **Start a new drawing using the Interior Design drawing template that was created in Chapter 8.**

49. **Open Design Center and find the Hotel Suite drawing you just saved. Highlight Layers in the Tree View. The preview pane shows all the layers that were created for the Hotel Suite.**

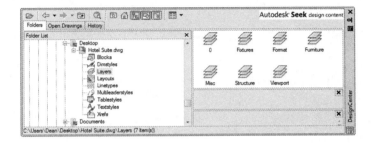

50. **Either double-left-click or click-and-drag each layer (except layer 0) into your drawing. When you are done, close the Design Center.**

51. **Verify that the layers came in by opening the Layer Manager.**

52. **Pick the Plan View tab and switch to Paper Space.**

53. **Use a Selection Window or a Crossing Window to select the drawing format with the titleblock. The grips will appear. Use the pull-down arrow on the Layers toolbar and pick layer Format. This changes all the selected objects to layer Format. Use the Escape key to eliminate the grips. Repeat this method to change the viewport border to layer Viewport.**

54. **Over-write the existing template: Pick File, Save As… and pick the Interior Design template to save the changes to the template. You will get a warning that it already exists. Pick Yes. Pick OK for Template Options.**

Congratulations! You have now updated the Interior Design template drawing to include layers.

Notes:

Chapter 11
Commands – Set 5: Annotating Your Drawing

Learning Objectives:

- **Creating a style and using Text**
- **Creating a style and using Dimensions**
- **Creating labels with the Multileader command**

We can now create accurate drawings. Unfortunately, this alone is not enough to convey the information you want to explain your design to a client or to a contractor. All drawings will need text and dimensions to identify what is drawn as well as the size and location of objects.

In this chapter, we will cover Text, Dimensions, and Multileader. The Multileader is the AutoCAD® name for a label.

Text

Putting text in your drawings is essential to identify items you have drawn or for notes you wish to make. AutoCAD® allows you to have Single Line text, or Multiline text. There is a default font available, but for Interior Design, a popular font is City Blueprint. We can create a custom Text Style and we will define the font.

Text Style

To begin, expand the Annotation Panel of the Home Tab, and pick the Text Style icon:

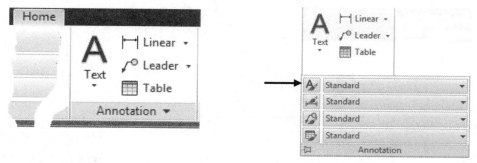

As an alternative, pick the downward arrow of the Text Panel of the Annotate Tab:

Pick the downward arrow

After selecting either the Text Style icon on the Annotation Panel of the Home Tab, or the downward arrow of the Text Panel of the Annotate Tab, the Text Style dialog box appears. We will create a new style by picking the New button.

The New Text Style dialog box appears with a default "style1" name, which is ready for editing to a name of your choosing. Let's choose "Notes". Type that in, and then pick OK.

Use the pull-down selection under "Font Name:" to select CityBlueprint as the fonts style. Once you pick the font, the Preview pane shows what the font looks like. Check off "Annotative" under the "Size" portion of the dialog box. Annotative text allows you to scale the text to your drawing so that you do not have to have multiple text styles at different heights. Set the "Paper Text Height" to 1/8″. When done, Pick the Apply button then Pick the Close button.

Leaving the height at 0″ will allow AutoCAD to prompt you for text height while placing text in your drawing. You can check out the difference by inserting Standard style Text and the Notes style just created.

For future use, let's create a second Text Style. Create a style that starts with Notes, but instead of a text height of 1/8″, use 1/4″ instead. Name that new style Titleblock.

Make sure Notes is highlighted before you pick the New button. The new style will be created with all the properties that that the Notes style has. When done, your dialog box will look like the following:

Select the Notes Style and Pick the Set Current button. Pick the Close button to exit the dialog box.

In the Text Panel, the current style is the one that is displayed. Ensure that the new style of Notes is the current style before you begin to use text. If it is not, use the pull-down arrow to choose it.

Annotate Tab

Home Tab

Use –pull down to choose Notes

Multiline Text

You can create multiple lines of text in a defined area. Before entering or importing text, you specify opposite corners of a text bounding box that defines the width of the paragraphs in the multiline text object. The length of the multiline text object depends on the amount of text, not the length of the bounding box. You can use grips to move or rotate a multiline text object.

Procedure:

Pick (left click): **Multiline Text icon** from the Annotation Panel of the Home Tab.
(As an alternative, use the Text Panel of the Annotate Tab)

The command line prompts you with the following:

Current text style: "Notes" Text height: 1/8" Annotative: Yes
MTEXT *Specify first corner:* **(Pick on your screen for first corner of bounding box)**

Specify opposite corner or [Height/Justify/Line spacing/Rotation/Style/Width/Columns]: **(Pick on your screen for the second corner of bounding box)**
After you define the bounding box for the text, a Text Editor Tab appears on your ribbon and a ruler appears above the bounding box you defined on your drawing screen:

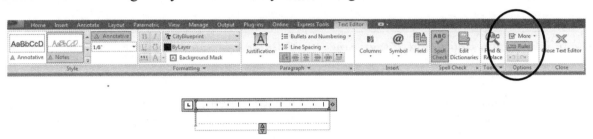

Type in the text you want in the bounding box. When you are done, pick Close Text Editor icon on the Text Editor Tab of the Ribbon.

Multiline text is useful for large amounts of text that is cut/pasted from a document. In addition, you have many options at your disposal with this command such as controlling formatting, special symbols, creating columns of text, etc. Otherwise, use Single Line Text.

Single Line Text

We will use the Single Line Text icon on the Annotate Panel of the Home Tab (or use the Text Panel of the Annotate Tab):

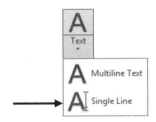

The Text icon is a fly-out. Once you pick Single Line Text as your command, it will remain visible, and Multiline Text will be hidden.

Procedure:

Pick (left click): **Single Line Text icon** from the Annotation Panel of the Home Tab.
        (As an alternative, use the Text Panel of the Annotate Tab)

The command line prompts you with the following:

Current text style: "Notes" Text height: 0'-0 1/8" Annotative: Yes
TEXT *Specify start point of text or [Justify/Style]:* **(Pick a point on the drawing to place the text)**

Specify rotation angle of text <0>: ↵   **Press the ↵ Enter key to accept the default angle. Key in your text. Your text will appear on the drawing.**

AutoCAD® allows additional lines of text; you press the ↵ Enter key to start the next line of text. When you are done entering text, **press the ↵ Enter key.**

If you only want a single line of text, press the ↵ Enter key twice to exit the command.

Note that if you were to place Annotative text onto your drawing while in the Model tab (or in a Layout tab if you haven't set/locked the scale), a dialog box will appear the first time you attempt to do this:

Using Annotative text is best done while you are working in a Layout tab in Model Space. Most times when you wish to apply text to your drawing, you want to apply it when you are laying-out your drawing for printing.

Prior to using Annotative text, set and lock the scale of your Model Space relative to the Paper Space. AutoCAD® will automatically scale the text for you.

AutoCAD does the scaling for you with Annotative text. If you are using a scale of ¼″=1′, your text height would have to be 48 times bigger to appear on the drawing.

Do the math: ¼″=1′ is the same as ¼″ = 12″ (the units need to be in inches for the math to work). Multiply both sides by 4 (to get rid of the fraction), you get 1″=48″. This means that to get a line of text to appear 3/16″ high on a drawing with a scale factor of ¼″=1′, the text would have to be drawn in the full-scale model 9″ high (3/16 x 48 =9).

As you can see, it is certainly convenient for AutoCAD® to do the math for us when it comes to getting the text to appear at the correct height on our layout.

Editing Text

For text that is already on your drawing that you wish to edit, you can double-click on it and it will allow you to edit it. Different text editing features are available depending on whether it is Single Line Text or Multiline Text.

Editing Single Line Text

After double-clicking the text, the command line will show the command, **_DDEDIT_ddedit,_** and the text that you double-clicked will highlight and allow you to begin editing. You can click within the text for specific character changes, or while the entire line of text is highlighted, you can type new text to completely replace it. The delete key on the keyboard can be used to delete characters as desired. Highlighting text and then typing will overwrite the text that was highlighted. After you finish editing, press the ↵ Enter key.

AutoCAD® will prompt you to select more text to edit. If you have none, press the ↵ Enter key to exit the command.

DDEDIT _Select an annotation object or [Undo]:_ ↵

Editing Multiline Text

After double-clicking the text, the command line will show the command, **_MTEDIT_mtedit,_** and the Text Editor Tab will appear on the ribbon. This is the same Text Editor that appeared when you were creating Multiline text. Editing of Multiline text is done in the same manner as single line text. When you are done, pick Close Text Editor icon on the Text Editor Tab of the Ribbon.

Relocating text

To relocate text on your drawing, it is easily done using grips with the Object Snap feature turned off. Simply pick the text to get the grip, and then pick the grip and move the text to the new location.

Special Characters

There are times when you need to insert a special character or symbol into your Single Line of text. Probably the most commonly used one would be the degree symbol "°".

You can insert a special character while inserting or editing text by keying in the correct code.

The following codes result in special characters:

Code	Resulting Character	Character Name
%%d	°	Degree Symbol
%%p	±	Plus/Minus Symbol
%%c	Ø	Diameter Symbol

Example:

Typing: "Door swings through 120%%d", results in "Door swings through 120°".

For Multiline text, you can add symbols and special characters directly from a list of choices. The list is found by using the Symbol icon, which is on the Insert Panel of the Text Editor Tab.

A listing of symbol choices will appear:

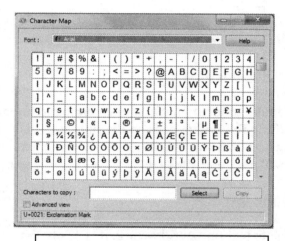

Picking Other… will bring up the Character Map. This will give many additional choices.

Scaling Text

For non-Annotative style text only, the text height can be changed using Scale Text. Pick the icon then pick the text you want to scale. The Scale Text icon is found by expanding the Text Panel of the Annotate Tab.

<u>Procedure:</u>

Pick (left click): **Scale Text icon** from the Text Panel of the Annotate Tab.

The command line prompts you with the following:

*SCALETEXT Select objects: (**Pick the text**)*
Select objects: 1 found ↵
Enter a base point option for scaling
[Existing/Left/Center/Middle/Right/TL/TC/TR/ML/MC/MR/BL/BC/BR] <Existing>: ↵
Specify new model height or [Paper height/Match object/Scale factor] <3/16">: **3/8** ↵
1 objects changed

You cannot change the scale of Annotative text. If you tried, your command line will advise:

1 annotative objects ignored

Dimensions

It is important to use dimensions in your drawing to describe the size and placement of items. AutoCAD® has a variety of dimensions available that can be customized. There are several types of dimensions: linear, aligned, radial, diameter, angular, etc. A standard style is available as the default style. This style is more suitable for engineering than it is for Interior Design. We will create a unique style that is better suited for use in Interior Design.

Dimension Style

To create a unique dimension style, expand the Annotation Panel of the Home Tab, and pick the Dimension Style icon.

As an alternative, pick the downward arrow of the Dimensions Panel of the Annotate Tab:

Pick the downward arrow

The Dimension Style Manager dialog box will appear.

The current dimension
style is identified here.

A preview of the
current dimension
style is shown here.

The list of
available
styles is
shown here.

To create a new dimension style, pick the New… button. A new dialog box will appear. Under New Style Name, the text "Copy of Standard" is highlighted and ready for editing. Let's name the new style Interior Design. Also, check-off Annotative.

After changing the name, pick the Continue button. A New Dimension Style dialog box will appear. There are seven tabs to choose in this dialog box. Pick the Primary Units tab (if it is not the currently displayed tab). It is here that we will change to architectural units by using the pull-down arrow of Unit format under the Linear Dimensions section on the left side of the dialog box.

Make the following change:
- Change Unit Format to Architectural

Notice the preview pane shows how the dimensions will appear. That is all we will change in the Primary Units tab. We will leave the Angular dimensions as Decimal Degrees with a zero precision.

Next, pick the Lines tab. It is here we can control the dimension lines and extension lines.

Make the following changes (if these values are not already there):
- Change the value of Baseline spacing to 3/8.
- Change the value of Extend beyond dim lines to 3/32 (You will need to type this value).
- Change the value of Offset from origin to 1/16.
- Change all Color and Lineweights from ByBlock to ByLayer

When done, your dialog box should look like this:

Now, pick the Symbols and Arrows tab. It is here we will control the style and size of the arrowheads.

Make the following changes under the Arrowheads portion of the dialog box:
- Change the arrow style to Architectural tick under both First and Second.
- Change the Arrow size to 1/16.

When done, your dialog box should look like this:

Pick the Text tab. We will change the appearance and placement of the text. For the alignment, we will leave the default value of Horizontal.

In the Text Appearance portion of the dialog box, make the following changes:
- Change the Text style to Notes (if you have not already created this style, you must create that first before this can be done)
- Change the Text color to ByLayer

In the Text Placement portion of the dialog box, make the following change:
- Change the value of Offset from dim line to 1/16

When done, your dialog box should look like this:

Note that the Text height becomes grayed-out because the Text style of Notes already has a Text height value of 1/8″.

Next, pick the Fit tab. We will change the Scale and Fine Tuning and leave the Options and Placement at the default values.

In the Scale for dimension features portion, Annotative should already be checked because the Text Style chosen is an Annotative style.

In the Fine Tuning portion, pick the check boxes for both items available. This will allow us to place the dimension text where we want it (instead of AutoCAD® automatically placing it) and it will draw the dimension lines between extension lines (primarily handy for radius and diameter dimensions).

When you are done making these changes, your dialog box will look like this:

Since these are the only changes we plan to make for our new dimension style, pick the OK button to exit the dialog box. AutoCAD® will return you to the Dimension Style Manager dialog box.

Ensure that Interior Design is the current dimension style. If it is not, pick it to highlight it (on the left side of the dialog box), and then pick the Set Current button. When done, pick the Close button to exit the dialog box.

Using Dimensions

It is important to use dimensions in your drawing to describe the size and placement of items. There are several types of dimensions: linear, aligned, angular, radius, diameter, etc. Icons for each type are available by using the fly-out icon in either the Annotation Panel of the Home Tab, or the Dimension Panel of the Annotate Tab.

You have just created a new dimension style. These instructions will show you how to use the various dimension icons.

As an example of using dimensions, download the file *Faucet.dwg* from the publisher website and open the drawing. We will dimension the faucet:

Before beginning to use the dimensions, ensure that OSNAP is turned on and the settings are logical for what you plan to select (example: Endpoint or Intersection). The faucet drawing already has the Text and Dimension styles we just created. Make sure that Interior Design is the Current style.

If you are working this example in the Model tab (or in a Layout tab without the Model Scale set and locked) the Select Annotation Scale dialog box will appear. You may choose the annotation scale by using the pull-down arrow. For this example, we will leave it at 1:1.

Linear Dimension

Linear dimensions are used to define the horizontal or vertical distances.

Procedure:

Pick (left click): **Linear Dimension icon** from the Annotation Panel of the Home Tab.
         (As an alternative, use the Dimension Panel of the Annotate Tab)

The command line prompts you with the following:

DIMLINEAR Specify first extension line origin or <select object>: **(Pick endpoint A)**

Specify second extension line origin: **(Pick endpoint B)**

Specify dimension line location or [Mtext/Text/Angle/Horizontal/Vertical/Rotated]: **(Pick a location for the dimension text)**

Dimension text = 1 1/4"

Aligned Dimension

Procedure:

Pick (left click): **Aligned Dimension icon** from the Annotation Panel of the Home Tab.
(As an alternative, use the Dimension Panel of the Annotate Tab)

The command line prompts you with the following:

DIMALIGNED *Specify first extension line origin or <select object>:* ***(Pick intersection point C)***

Specify second extension line origin: ***(Pick endpoint D)***

Specify dimension line location or
[Mtext/Text/Angle]: ***(Pick a location for the dimension text)***

Dimension text = 1/2"

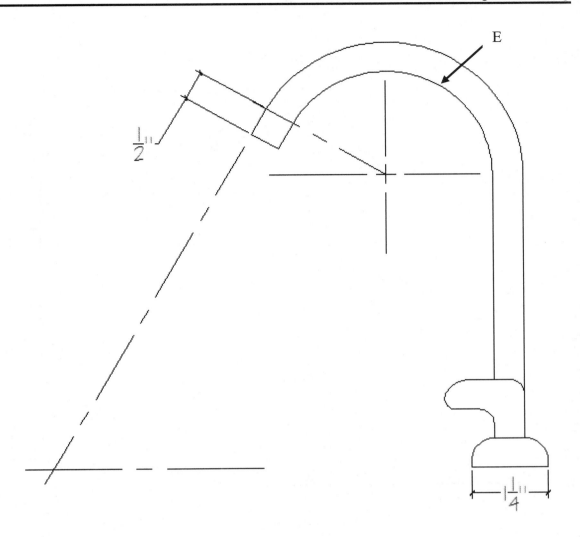

Radius Dimension

Procedure:

Pick (left click): **Radius Dimension icon** from the Annotation Panel of the Home Tab.
       (As an alternative, use the Dimension Panel of the Annotate Tab)

The command line prompts you with the following:

*DIMRADIUS Select arc or circle: **(Pick arc E)***

Dimension text = 1 3/4"
*Specify dimension line location or [Mtext/Text/Angle]: **(Pick a location for the dimension text)***

Angular Dimension

Procedure:

Pick (left click): **Angular Dimension icon** from the Annotation Panel of the Home Tab.
(As an alternative, use the Dimension Panel of the Annotate Tab)

The command line prompts you with the following:

*DIMANGULAR Select arc, circle, line, or <specify vertex>: **(Pick line F)***

*Select second line: **(Pick line G)***

*Specify dimension arc line location or [Mtext/Text/Angle]: **(Pick a location for the dimension text)***

Dimension text = 60

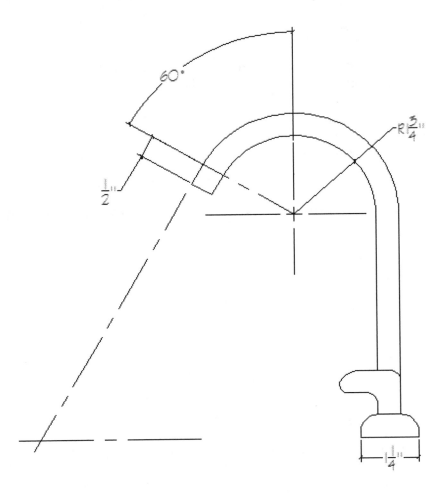

Diameter Dimension

As an example for this dimension type, we will use a simple 4″ diameter circle.

<u>Procedure:</u>

Pick (left click): **Diameter Dimension icon** from the Annotation Panel of the Home Tab.
      (As an alternative, use the Dimension Panel of the Annotate Tab)

The command line prompts you with the following:

DIMDIAMETER *Select arc or circle:* ***(Pick the circle)***

Dimension text = 4"
Specify dimension line location or [Mtext/Text/Angle]: ***(Pick a location for the dimension text)***

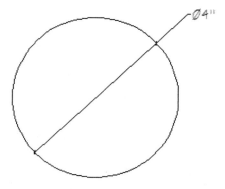

The default setting for AutoCAD® diameter dimension is to use the diameter symbol: ⌀.

We can change that by modifying the existing style. Pick the Dimension Style icon. When the Dimension Style Manager dialog box appears, select the New button.

In the Create New Dimension Style dialog box, use the pull-down arrow under Use for: to select the Diameter dimensions, then pick the Continue button.

When the New Dimension Style dialog box appears, select the Primary Units tab.

Change the Prefix text by typing a space (you won't be able to see it). Change the Suffix text by typing a space and the word DIA. Notice how it changes in the preview pane. Pick the OK button when you are done.

AutoCAD® returns to the Dimension Style Manager dialog box. Notice that the new diameter style that was just created is a subset of the dimension style Interior Design.

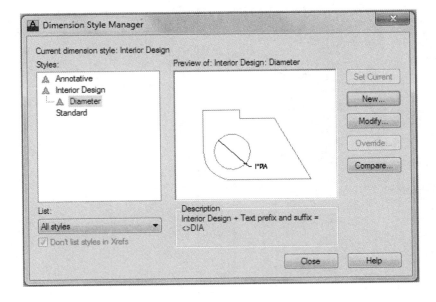

Now when a diameter dimension is created using the style Interior Design, the diameter dimension will look like this:

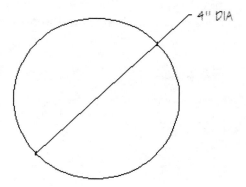

Modifying Existing Dimensions

There are times when dimensions share the same extension lines. Rather than create a unique style with the dimension line suppressed, this can be accomplished by using the Properties Palette. In the Properties Palette, after the dimension is selected, either extension line 1 or 2 or both can be turned off.

This example shows the Properties Palette was used to turn Ext line 2 off.

Multileader

To label items on your drawing, use a Multileader. The Multileader can have an arrow with line and text. You can create a unique Multileader style in a similar way that we created a unique dimension style.

Multileader Style

To create a unique Multileader style, expand the Annotation Panel of the Home Tab, and pick the Multileader Style icon.

As an alternative, pick the downward arrow of the Leaders Panel of the Annotate Tab:

Pick the downward arrow

The Multileader Style Manager dialog box will appear.

The current Multileader style is identified here.

A preview of the current Multileader style is shown here.

The list of available styles is shown here.

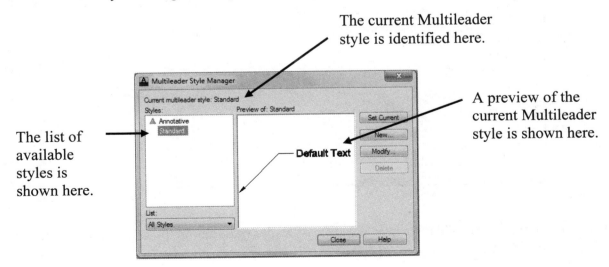

To create a new Multileader style, pick the New… button. A new dialog box will appear. Under New Style Name, the text "Copy of Standard" is highlighted and ready for editing. Let's name the new style Label. Also, check-off Annotative. Pick the Continue button when done.

A Modify Multileader Style dialog box will appear. This is where you will make the setting changes. There are three tabs to choose from. Pick the Content tab.

Make the following changes under the Content tab:

- Change the Text style to Notes (as created in previous chapter)
- Change the Text color from ByBlock to ByLayer

When done, your dialog box should look like this:

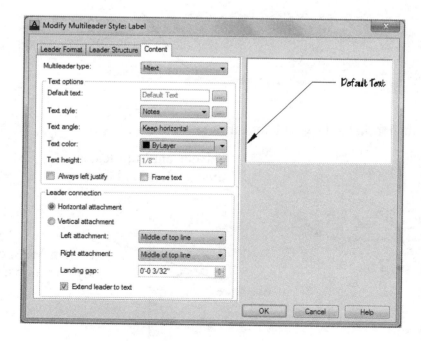

Pick the Leader Format tab. This is where the style of leader (straight or spline), and the choice of multiple arrowheads are made.

The following shows the difference between a Straight Leader and a Spline Leader:

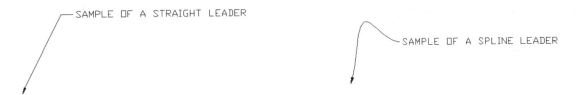

For this style, we will leave the Type as Straight.

The multiple arrowhead choices are found by using the pull-down arrow in the Arrowhead section of the dialog box:

For this style, we will leave the Arrowhead Symbol as Closed filled.
Make the following changes under the Leader Format tab:

- Change the Arrowhead Size to 1/4.
- Change ByBlock to ByLayer for all items.

When done, your dialog box should look like this:

Pick the Leader Structure tab. Each line segment can be constrained as you desire.

Make the following changes under the Leader Structure tab:

- Change the landing distance to 1/4.

When done, your dialog box should look like this:

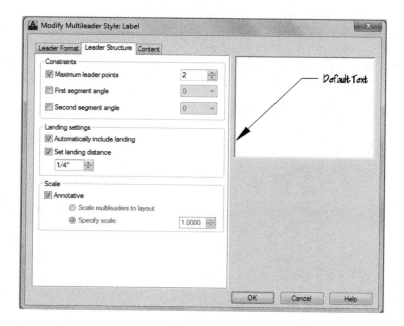

Note that if you desired, you can change the Maximum number of leader points. Below is an example of 3 leader points:

Example of 3 leader points

Pick OK to exit the dialog box. Pick Close to exit the Multileader Style Manager dialog box. The current style should now be set to Label:

Inserting a Multileader on Your Drawing

Procedure:

Pick (left click): **Multileader icon** from the Annotation Panel of the Home Tab.
(As an alternative, use the Leaders Panel of the Annotate Tab)

The command line prompts you with the following:

MLEADER *Specify leader arrowhead location or [leader Landing first/Content first/Options] <Options>:* **(Pick the object that you are adding a label to. This will be the Arrow end of the first segment. This may be an endpoint or midpoint, or somewhere close to the object with OSNAP off)**

Specify leader landing location: **(Pick a location for the end of the arrow)**

As soon as you pick the leader landing location, the Text Editor Panel will appear on the ribbon. Also, a flashing I-bar will appear near the leader landing. This is where you type in the information for your Multileader (label).

(Key in the desired text).

When you are done typing in the text, pick the Close Text Editor icon on the Text Editor Panel. This will close the dialog box and exit the command.

As an example, let's assume we are labeling a coffee table. When done, your Multileader should look like this:

Summary

In this chapter you have learned to:

- Create different styles of text
- Create a style for dimensions that is suitable for interior design
- Use various types of dimensions, including linear, aligned, radial and angular
- Modify existing dimensions
- Create a label style for Multileader
- Use Multileaders for labeling objects

Review Questions

1. What does "Annotative" style mean?

2. What does "current style" mean?

3. What does a text height of 0″ mean?

4. What are the differences between Single Line Text and Multiline Text?

5. What is an easy way to relocate text on your drawing?

6. After text is already on the drawing, how can you change it's size?

7. What is the difference between a dimension line and an extension line?

8. What is an easy method to turn a dimension extension line off?

9. How do you change the default diameter symbol?

10. What is a Spline Leader?

Exercises

1. Draw the bookshelf. Use the 8-1/2″ x 11″ layout to set and lock the scale to 1″ = 1′. Create layers "Object", "Viewport", and "Dimension and Text". Set the Lineweight of layer Object to .012″. Place the viewport border on layer Viewport and Freeze the layer. The bookshelf is drawn on layer Object. Use the dimension, text, and multileader styles created in this chapter. The dimensions and multileaders must be Model Space objects and placed on the Dimensions and Text layer. The text items are Paper Space objects and belong on Dimensions and Text layer.

2. Draw the Hinge and Screw Detail. Use Paper Space with two viewports – one for the hinge the other for the screw detail. Set the scale for the hinge viewport to 1:1 and the screw detail to 4:1. Dimension the hinge and the screw detail – make sure to use the annotative dimension style you created in this chapter.

3. Draw the country hutch. Use the drawing format sheet, layers, dimensions, text, multileaders, and create viewports and layouts.
    The hutch drawing details are on the following three drawing sheets:
    (Hint for side view: draw the arcs as circles, draw a line tangent to the circles for the angled line (use Snap-to-Tangent), and trim the circles so they become arcs).

Notes:

Chapter 12
Hotel Suite Project – Tutorial 5

Learning Objectives:

- **To continue creating a drawing of a real-world application of AutoCAD®**
  - o **Create an elevation view**
  - o **Annotate with Text, Dimensions, and Multileader**
  - o **Create multiple layouts**
- **To utilize and reinforce the use of the AutoCAD® commands learned in the previous chapters**
- **Update the Template drawing**

This tutorial builds on Tutorial 4 found in Chapter 10. In this tutorial, we will create an elevation view of the bedroom. We will also create additional layers and annotate the drawing. When you are finished with this tutorial, the bedroom elevation will be completed and you will have dimensions, labels, and text your printable 8-1/2″x 11″ sheets.

In addition, we will update our template drawing to include Text, Dimension, and Multileader styles.

Commands & Techniques:

- Opening an existing drawing
- Zoom
- Pan
- Construction Line
- Trim
- Design Center
- Line
- Object Snap
- Move
- Erase
- Offset
- Fillet
- Text Style
- Single Line Text
- Grips
- Create new Layout
- Dimension
- Multiline Text
- Multileader
- Save

Create an Elevation View

Before beginning, open the Hotel Suite drawing that you updated in Tutorial 4. Note, for this tutorial, the author has changed the colors of the layers back to white and hidden the lineweights to make it easier to see in the textbook. Make sure layer "Structure" is the current layer.

We will draw this elevation.

We will draw the elevation view of the bedroom as shown above. As you already know from drawing elevation views by hand, the best way to start the new view is to project from the plan view. In AutoCAD®, the projection lines will be construction lines.

1. Create vertical construction lines to project below the plan view.

> You do not need to project all the lines. In fact, for the utility closet, it is best to project the midpoint instead of the endpoints because the access panel will cover the opening. The same is recommended for aligning the furniture – project the midpoints of the desk and dresser instead of the endpoints.

Vertical construction lines are used to project either endpoints or midpoints (as appropriate) from the plan view into the elevation view.

We will build the elevation view directly below the plan view. Leave some space between the plan and elevation views. It is important to note that the ceiling height is 8′.

2. Create a horizontal construction line a reasonable distance below the plan view.

This horizontal construction line will represent the ceiling of the room in the elevation view.

3. Offset the horizontal construction line 8′ down.

This offset construction line will represent the floor of the room in the elevation view.

4. Use the Trim command to trim all the construction lines.

After trimming, your drawing will look like this:

Adding the Blocks to the Drawing

Prior to inserting the block, you must have the Hotel Suite Blocks – Bedroom Elevation drawing that you can download from the publisher's web site.

The Blocks that we are going to use for the bedroom elevation view are shown below:

Adding Blocks to the Bedroom Elevation

Let's insert the blocks one at a time. Before inserting the furniture blocks, make sure layer "Furniture" is the current layer.

5. Use Design Center to insert the Dresser block.

6. Use the Line command to draw a line between the legs of the dresser.

> Because the dresser needs to be aligned with the projection line, we need to locate the center. The reason for adding a line between the legs of the dresser is because the dresser must set on the floor.

7. Use the Move command to relocate the dresser from the midpoint of the line created in step 6 to the endpoint of the projection line.

> Pick only the Dresser block, not the line.

8. Use the Erase command to erase the line created in step 6 and the projection line.

When you are done, your elevation view will look like this:

9. Use Design Center to insert the Desk & Chair block.

10. Use the Line command to draw a line between the legs of the desk.

Because the desk needs to be aligned with the projection line, we need to locate the center. The reason for adding a line between the legs of the desk is because the desk must set on the floor.

11. Use the Move command to relocate the desk from the midpoint of the line created in step 10 to the endpoint of the projection line.

Pick only the Desk & Chair block, not the line.

12. Use the Erase command to erase the line created in step 10 and the projection line.

When you are done, your elevation view will look like this:

The bottom of the louver doors is 1″ above the floor to provide adequate clearance for opening and closing. Before we bring in the block for the doors, we will create the location off the floor. In addition, we will change the current layer to "Structure".

13. Offset the floor 1″ upward.

14. Trim the offset line between the door opening.

Offset line is trimmed
between the projection lines
of the closet door opening.

15. Use Design Center to insert the Louver Doors block.

16. Use the Line command to draw a line at the bottom and between the two middle doors.

Because the doors must be centered in the opening and above the floor, we need to locate the center.

Line added between middle doors at the bottom of the Louver Doors block.

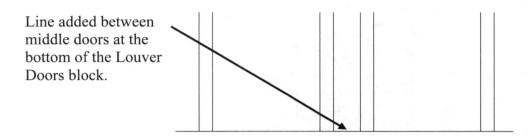

17. Use the Move command to relocate the doors from the midpoint of the line created in step 16 to the midpoint of the line created in step 14.

Pick only the Louver Doors block, not the line.

18. Use the Erase command to erase the lines created in steps 14 and 16.

When you are done, your elevation view will look like this:

There is a 1/2″ clearance at the top of the louver doors. We will draw that in next.

19. Create a horizontal construction line at the top of the louver doors.

Snap to any endpoint of the lines at the top of the louver doors.

20. Offset the construction line 1/2″ upward.

21. Erase the construction line created in step 19.

22. Use the Fillet command with a radius of 0″ to close out the projection lines and the offset construction line.

When you are done, the top of the louver door opening will look like this:

23. Use Design Center to insert the Access Panel block.

Because the bottom of the access panel is 5″ off the floor, we will need to create an offset line from the floor.

24. Use the Offset command to offset the floor 5″ upward.

25. Use the Move command to relocate the Access Panel.

Snap to the Midpoint of the bottom horizontal line of the access panel and to the intersection of the projection line and the offset line created in step 24.

26. Use the Erase command to erase the line created in step 24.

For now, we will keep the projection line. We will need it to locate the thermostat.

When you are done, your elevation view will look like this:

27. Use Design Center to insert the Thermostat block.

The thermostat is located on the same centerline as the access panel and the bottom of the thermostat is 2″ above the access panel. We will need to create a line offset 2″ above the top of the access panel.

28. Create a horizontal construction line at the top of the access panel.

29. Offset the construction line 2″ upward.

30. Erase the construction line created in step 28.

31. Use the Move command to relocate the Thermostat.

Snap to the Midpoint of the bottom of the thermostat to the Intersection of the construction line of step 29 and the projection line.

32. Use the Erase command to erase the projection line and the line created in step 29.

When you are done, your elevation view will look like this:

Before we insert the Flat Screen TV block, change the active layer to "Misc".

33. Use the Design Center to insert the Flat Screen TV block.

34. Use the Move command to relocate the TV to the top of the dresser.

Snap to the Midpoint of the bottom of the TV to the Midpoint of the top of the dresser.

When you are done, your elevation view will look like this:

Layout the Drawing

Before we begin a layout of the bedroom elevation, we should fill out the titleblock that was created for the Plan View layout tab in Tutorial 4.

35. Create text styles so that we can fill in the titleblock.

(Pick the Text Styles icon)

The Text Style dialog box appears:

(Pick the New button)

The New Text Style dialog box appears:

Key in the name "Titleblock"   *(Pick the OK button when done)*

36. Use the pull down arrows to select the font of **Times New Roman** for the **Font Name** and **Bold Italic** for the **Font Style.** Place a check mark for **Annotative.**

We will leave the Height at 0″ so that we can key in the value as we place the text on the drawing.

37. While still in the **Text Style** dialog box, we will create an additional style and name it **"Notes".** The new style will have the following properties:

> Font: CityBlueprint
> Annotative: yes – place a check mark in the box
> Text Height: 1/8″

38. While in the **Plan View** layout tab, place **Single Line** text in the titleblock as shown:

Make sure you are in Paper Space before you attempt to insert text.

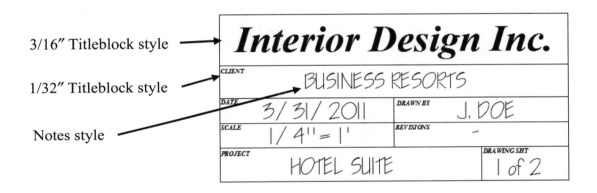

3/16″ Titleblock style

1/32″ Titleblock style

Notes style

38a. Use the pull-down arrow on the **Text Style** portion of the **Annotation Panel** of the **Home Tab** to make **Titleblock** the current style.

38b. Use the **Single Line Text** command on the **Annotation Panel** of the **Home Tab** to insert the company name in the titleblock.

(Pick the Single Line Text icon)

Current text style: "Titleblock" Text height: 0'-0 3/16" Annotative: Yes
*TEXT Specify start point of text or [Justify/Style]: (**Pick a location in the titleblock**)*
Specify height <0'-0 3/16">: ⏎
Specify rotation angle of text <0>: ⏎

Key in the text "Interior Design Inc." and press the ↵ Enter key twice to exit the command.

38c. **Use Single Line Text to insert the remaining titleblock text which is all capital letters.**

Press the ↵ Enter key to repeat the Single Line Text command.

Current text style: "Titleblock" Text height: 0'-0 3/16" Annotative: Yes
*TEXT Specify start point of text or [Justify/Style]: **(Pick a location in the titleblock)***
Specify height <0'-0 3/16">: **1/32** ↵
Specify rotation angle of text <0>: ↵

Key in the text to fill in the remainder of the titleblock. Press the ↵ Enter key twice to exit the command.

38d. **Use the pull-down arrow in the Text Style section of the Annotation Panel of the Home Tab to change the current Text Style to Notes.**

38e. **Complete the titleblock.**

The text you placed in the titleblock may not be placed exactly where you want it. Use grips to relocate the text. Turn off Object Snap before moving the text around.

38f. **Change the layer that the titleblock and format border rectangle are on to layer "Format"**

Now that we have the titleblock in the Plan View layout filled out, we can create another layout for the bedroom elevation view.

39. **Create a layout for the bedroom elevation view.**

(Right-click the Plan View tab)

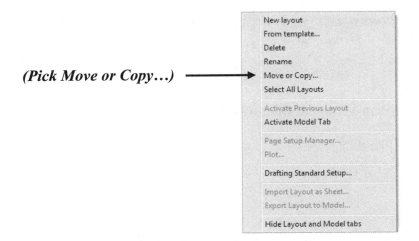

(Pick Move or Copy…)

After the Move or Copy dialog box appears:

(Pick move to end)

(Pick in the check box to Create a copy)

(Pick the OK button when you are done)

40. Rename the new layout tab to "Bedroom Elevation".

41. While in the Bedroom Elevation layout tab, switch to Model Space.

42. Unlock the viewport scale and pan the view of your model so that you center the bedroom elevation. Change the scale to 1/2″ = 1′, and lock the viewport scale.

If the plan view is still showing in the viewport, switch back to Paper Space and re-size the viewport so that only the bedroom elevation view is showing. Leave enough empty space around it to allow for dimensions and text.

43. Switch back to Paper Space and edit the scale and sheet number in the titleblock.

The text for scale should read: 1/2″ = 1′
The text for the sheet number should read: 2 of 2

(Double-click on the text to edit)

*DDEDIT Select an annotation object or [Undo]: **(Pick the text and edit it)** ↵*
Select an annotation object or [Undo]:↵

44. Delete the Layout 2 tab.

You will now have two layouts – Plan View and Bedroom Elevation.

Your Plan View layout will look like this:

Your Bedroom Elevation layout will look like this:

Notice that the viewport border is visible. When you print your drawing, it is not desirable to have the viewport border on the printout. We cannot delete it because it will leave us with a blank drawing. To get around this, we can create a unique layer and we can freeze the layer from visibility.

45. For each layout, if it is not already done, change the layer that the viewport is currently on, to layer Viewport.

46. For each layout, use the pull-down arrow on the Layers Panel of the Home Tab to freeze layer Viewport.

You must be in Paper Space before you freeze layer Viewport.

(Pick the Freeze or thaw in current viewport icon for layer Viewport)

<u>Annotating the Drawing</u>

We are done setting up the drawing layouts. We can now annotate the drawing with dimensions and labels. First, we will need to create styles for both Dimensions and Multileader. We will use the same styles that we created in Chapter 11. The steps to creating those styles will not be repeated here. Please refer to that chapter to create the styles. Otherwise, import them using Design Center.

Before you begin, create a new layer and name it "Dimensions and Text", and make it current.

47. Add two linear dimensions to the plan view.

Make sure you are in the Plan View layout tab and working in Model Space with Object Snap set to Endpoint.

(Pick the Linear icon on the Annotation Panel of the Home Tab)

DIMLINEAR *Specify first extension line origin or <select object>:*
(Pick one of the endpoints for the horizontal dimension at the top of the drawing)

Specify second extension line origin:
(Pick the other endpoint for the horizontal dimension)

Specify dimension line location or
[Mtext/Text/Angle/Horizontal/Vertical/Rotated]: *(Pick a location for the dimension text)*
Dimension text = 36'-8 1/2"

Press the ↵ Enter key to repeat the command.

DIMLINEAR *Specify first extension line origin or <select object>:*
(Pick one of the endpoints for the vertical dimension at the side of the drawing)

Specify second extension line origin:
(Pick the other endpoint for the vertical dimension)

Specify dimension line location or
[Mtext/Text/Angle/Horizontal/Vertical/Rotated]: *(Pick a location for the dimension text)*
Dimension text = 13'-6 3/4"

Creating a View Symbol Block

The symbol can be created as a triangle that surrounds a 3/16 diameter circle.

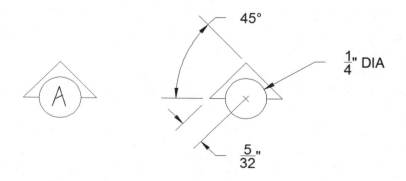

We will create a view symbol as a Model Space object and convert it to an annotative style Block. Because we are making it annotative, it will take on the correct scale on your layout.

48. Create the view symbol:

48a. Select the Model tab and zoom in on a blank area of your drawing.

48b. Draw a circle that is 1/4″ diameter.

48c. Draw a horizontal construction line through the center of the circle

48d. Draw two angled construction lines through the center of the circle: one at 45º and one at -45 º.

49e. Offset the angled construction lines 5/32″ up.

49f. Erase the original angled construction lines created in step 48d.

49g. Trim the construction lines.

49h. Use Single Line Text to insert the symbol text. Turn off Object Snap and use grips to position the text where it looks best.

Make sure text style is set to Notes.

49i. **Create a Block of the view symbol. Select Annotative in the Block Definition dialog box. Turn Object Snap back on and select the center of the circle as the Base point. Type the name "View Symbol".**

50. **Add Multiline Text to the Plan View layout as a Paper Space object.**

    Using 1/4″ Bold letters, type the words "PLAN VIEW".

51. **Add labels to the elevation view by using Multileader.**

52. Add Multiline Text to the Bedroom Elevation layout as a Paper Space object.

   Using 1/4″ Bold letters, type the words "ELEVATION A".

Congratulations! You have now completed all the tutorials. Be sure to save your drawing.

Your two drawing sheets will now look like this:

Add a Block and Text, Dimension, and Multileader Styles to Template

Let's take advantage of the various styles and the Block we created in this tutorial and build them into our drawing template.

53. **Start a new drawing using the Interior Design drawing template that was updated in Chapter 10.**

54. **Open Design Center Palette and find the Hotel Suite drawing you just saved.**

   54a. **Highlight Textstyles in the Tree View. The preview pane shows all the text styles that were created for the Hotel Suite, in addition to Standard and Annotative. Double-left-click, or click-and-drag the "Notes", and "Titleblock" styles to bring them into the template.**

   54b. **Highlight Dimstyles in the Tree View. The preview pane shows all the Dimension styles that were created for the Hotel Suite, in addition to Standard and Annotative. Double-left-click, or click-and-drag the "Interior Design" as well as the sub-set to "Interior Design" style, to bring them into the template.**

   54c. **Highlight Multileaderstyles in the Tree View. The preview pane shows all the Multileader styles that were created for the Hotel Suite, in addition to Standard and Annotative. Double-left-click, or click-and-drag the "Label" style, to bring it into the template.**

   54d. **Highlight Blocks in the Tree View. The preview pane shows all the Blocks that are part of the Hotel Suite. Double-left-click the View Symbol. Pick Cancel in the Insert Block dialog box. This method places the Block definition into the drawing without placing the Block in the drawing space.**

   54e. **Close the Design Center Palette.**

55. **Use Save As… and save the template as "Interior Design". Pick Yes to the warning and OK to the Template Option dialog boxes.**

Congratulations! You have now updated the Interior Design template drawing to include Text, Dimension, and Multileader styles in addition to the View Pointer Block!

Chapter 13
Commands – Set 6: Creating and Editing Schedules

Paint Schedule			
Room	Walls	Ceiling	Trim & Doors
Dining Room	California Paints Tomahawk Red, 7856A Latex, Eggshell Finish	Glidden Paints Ceiling Whitec GC3070 Latex	Benjamin Moore Navajo White, N31973 Acrylic, Eggshell Finish
Living Room	Behr Paints Forest Green Latex, Eggshell Finish	Glidden Paints Ceiling Whitec GC3070 Latex	Benjamin Moore Navajo White, N31973 Acrylic, Eggshell Finish

Learning Objectives:

- Creating a style for your Schedule using Table Style
- Use the Table feature to create a Schedule
- Edit an existing Table

Tables – Creating a Schedule

You can create a schedule by using the AutoCAD® Table command. Tables can have any number of rows and columns that you define. Defining a Table Style allows you to customize how the table will look.

Creating a Table Style

To begin, expand the Annotation Panel of the Home Tab, and pick the Table Style icon:

As an alternative, pick the downward arrow of the Tables Panel of the Annotate Tab:

Pick the downward arrow

After selecting either the Table Style icon on the Annotation Panel of the Home Tab, or the downward arrow of the Tables Panel of the Annotate Tab, the Table Style dialog box appears. We will create a new style by picking the New button.

Pick the New button in the dialog box and a Create New Table Style dialog box will appear. Let's create a style named Schedule:

Pick the Continue button. Another dialog box will appear. This dialog box will allow you to define several features for your Table Style.

Properties for each section are controlled using the choices within each of these three tabs.

Each section is selected by using pull-down under Cell styles.

There are three sections to the table: Title, Header, and Data. This is illustrated in the preview pane.

There are three sections that comprise the AutoCAD® schedule: Title, Header, and Data. These can each have their own properties for Alignment and Color, Text Style, and Border style. Each section is selected by using the pull-down under Cell styles. Once selected, the properties for that section are controlled using the tabs General, Text, and Borders.

Prior to choosing the style of text for each section, we need to have a style already defined. Previously, we created a style and named it Notes. We also set the text height for Notes to 1/8″. Notice that the Title text height is larger than the Header and Data text heights. By setting the text height in Text Style, we are not able to change that height to a larger size for the Title section. That is why we created the second style: Titleblock.

Table Title

Use the pull-down to select Title under Cell styles.

We will not make any changes under the General tab.
Pick the Text tab and make the following changes:

- Change the Text style to Titleblock.
- Change the Text color from ByBlock to ByLayer.

When done your changes are reflected in the preview panes and your dialog box will now look like the following:

Pick the Borders tab and make the following changes:

- Change ByBlock to ByLayer for all choice selections.
- Pick the left-most button for the grid border.

When done, your dialog box will now look like the following:

Table Header

Use the pull-down to select Header under Cell styles.

Pick the Text tab and make the following changes:

- Change the Text style to Notes.
- Change the Text color from ByBlock to ByLayer.

When done, the dialog box will now look like the following:

Pick the Borders tab and make the same changes for Header as you did for the Title style:

- Change ByBlock to ByLayer for all choice selections.
- Pick the left-most button for the grid border.

Table Data

Use the pull-down to select Data under Cell styles.

Pick the Text tab and make the same changes for Data that you made for the Header style:
- Change the Text style to Notes.
- Change the Text color from ByBlock to ByLayer.

Pick the Borders tab and make the same changes for Data as you did for both the Header and Title styles:

- Change ByBlock to ByLayer for all choice selections.
- Pick the left-most button for the grid border.

The table style of Schedule is now complete. Pick the OK button to exit the New Table Style dialog box and return to the Table Style dialog box. Pick the Schedule Style on the left side of the dialog box, and then pick the Set Current button to make it the current style. Pick the Close button to exit the dialog box.

The current style should now be set to Schedule:

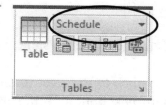

Inserting Tables on the Drawing

To insert a table on the drawing, it is best done on the Layout tab in Paper Space.

Procedure:

Pick (left click): **Table icon** from the Annotation Panel of the Home Tab.
         (As an alternative, use the Tables Panel of the Annotate Tab)

The Insert Table dialog box will appear. In this dialog box, the number of rows and columns can be specified, as well as the height and width of the rows and columns. For this example, change the number of columns to 3. Pick the OK button to insert the table.

An image of the table will appear on the screen and will follow the cursor. Left-click to place the table in a desired location on the drawing sheet.

A Text Editor Tab will appear on the ribbon and a blank table will appear on the drawing space.

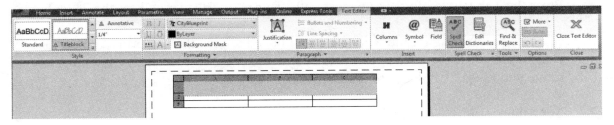

The cell that you will add text to will be highlighted. Enter the text as desired.
- To add lines within a cell, hold down the ALT key and press the Enter ↵ Key.
- To move to the next cell use the Tab key.

Try it:

We will create a schedule on the Layout 1 tab. The schedule will be a Paper Space object. Before we insert the Table, erase the viewport that is on Layout 1 – we will not need to see any part of our Model so we won't need any viewports.

Let's create the following paint schedule:

Paint Schedule		
<u>Walls</u>	<u>Ceiling</u>	<u>Trim & Doors</u>
California Paints Tomahawk Red, 7856A Latex, Eggshell Finish	Glidden Paints Ceiling White, GC 3070 Latex	Benjamin Moore Navajo White, N319 73 Acrylic, Eggshell Finish

1. For the Title section, Pick the Bold and Underline buttons on the Formatting Panel of the Text Editor Tab:

Bold

Underline

2. Type the words: **<u>Paint Schedule</u>**

3. Press the Tab key to move to the next cell. This is the Header cell for the 1st column.

4. Pick the Underline button.

5. Type the word: <u>Walls</u>

6. Press the Tab key to move to the next cell. This is the Header cell for the 2nd column.

7. Fill in the remaining Header cells. You will need to pick the Underline button for each Header cell. Use the tab key to change cells. After the last Header cell, the tab key will move you to the 1st column of the Data cell.

8. Type the words: California Paints

9. Hold the ALT key down and press the ↵ Enter Key. This allows you to create another line of text within the same cell. Repeat this for the third line of text.

10. Press the tab key to move to the next Data cell. Continue entering the information for all the cells.

11. Pick the Close Text Editor button to exit the command and complete the table.

Editing an Existing Table

If you simply want to add text to an existing cell, double-left-click inside the cell. The cell will highlight and the Text Editor Tab will appear. All methods used to enter information to the table are the same as when the table was initially created.

To edit an existing table, such as adding rows or columns, pick in a cell (single left click). The Table Cell Tab appears on the ribbon. It is here where you can make changes to the cells.

Try it:

Let's modify the Paint Schedule we just created by adding another column to identify the room that the paint scheme applies to:

1. *(Pick a cell in Column A of the Paint Schedule to make the Table Cell Tab appear)*
2. *(Pick Insert Left from the Columns Panel)*

A new column will appear to the left of the column labeled Walls.

1. *(Pick a cell in Row 3 of the Paint Schedule)*
2. *(Pick Insert Below from the Rows Panel)*

A new row will appear below the bottom row of the schedule.

Paint Schedule			
	Walls	Ceiling	Trim & Doors
	California Paints Tomahawk Red, 7856A Latex, Eggshell Finish	Glidden Paints Ceiling Whitec GC5070 Latex	Benjamin Moore Navajo White, N31973 Acrylic, Eggshell Finish

Let's title the new column as "Room". For the first row this will be for the "Dining Room". For the second row, this will be for the "Living Room". Remember to double-left click to edit the cells. For the living room we will keep the ceiling and trim and doors the same as the dining room, but we will make the walls a Behr Paints, Forest Green, Latex, Eggshell Finish. You can copy the cells for the ceiling and door paint colors by single clicking the cell that has the info, right click and select copy, and then single click the cell you want to add the information to and right click and select paste.

When you are done, your schedule will look like this:

Paint Schedule			
Room	Walls	Ceiling	Trim & Doors
Dining Room	California Paints Tomahawk Red, 7856A Latex, Eggshell Finish	Glidden Paints Ceiling Whitec GC3070 Latex	Benjamin Moore Navajo White, N31973 Acrylic, Eggshell Finish
Living Room	Behr Paints Forest Green Latex, Eggshell Finish	Glidden Paints Ceiling Whitec GC3070 Latex	Benjamin Moore Navajo White, N31973 Acrylic, Eggshell Finish

Notice that the columns are wider than they need to be. We can change the column widths and row heights by using grips. You can get the grips by using a single left-click on any cell.

Let's reduce the size of the first column:

(Pick in the cell that has the word <u>Room</u>)

	A	B	C	D
1		Paint Schedule		
2		Walls	Ceiling	Trim & Doors
3	Dining Room	California Paints Tomahawk Red, 7856A Latex, Eggshell Finish	Glidden Paints Ceiling White, GC 3070 Latex	Benjamin Moore Navajo White, N519 79 Acrylic, Eggshell Finish
4	Living Room	Behr Paints Forest Green Latex, Eggshell Finish	Glidden Paints Ceiling White, GC 3070 Latex	Benjamin Moore Navajo White, N519 79 Acrylic, Eggshell Finish

(Pick the right grip and drag it left to reduce the column width. Press the Esc key when done.)

When you are done, your Paint Schedule will look like this:

Paint Schedule			
Room	Walls	Ceiling	Trim & Doors
Dining Room	California Paints Tomahawk Red, 7856A Latex, Eggshell Finish	Glidden Paints Ceiling Whitec GC3070 Latex	Benjamin Moore Navajo White, N31973 Acrylic, Eggshell Finish
Living Room	Behr Paints Forest Green Latex, Eggshell Finish	Glidden Paints Ceiling Whitec GC3070 Latex	Benjamin Moore Navajo White, N31973 Acrylic, Eggshell Finish

You can continue to re-size each column and row until you are satisfied.

Paint Schedule			
<u>Room</u>	<u>Walls</u>	<u>Ceiling</u>	<u>Trim & Doors</u>
Dining Room	California Paints Tomahawk Red, 7856A Latex, Eggshell Finish	Glidden Paints Ceiling Whitec GC3070 Latex	Benjamin Moore Navajo White, N31973 Acrylic, Eggshell Finish
Living Room	Behr Paints Forest Green Latex, Eggshell Finish	Glidden Paints Ceiling Whitec GC3070 Latex	Benjamin Moore Navajo White, N31973 Acrylic, Eggshell Finish

Summary

In this chapter you have learned to:

- Create a Table Style
- Create a schedule using the Table command
- Add and Edit Text for a Table
- Modify an existing Table by adding and re-sizing columns or rows

Review Questions

1. What does AutoCAD® call Schedules?

2. Why is it better to make a schedule in Paper Space than Model Space?

3. Where can you find the Table Style icon?

4. Which toolbar has the Table command icon?

5. To edit text on an existing Table, how do you get the text editor?

6. How do you add a row or a column to an existing Table?

7. How do you change the size of a column or row in a Table?

Exercises

1. Create the following Door and Hardware Schedule in Paper Space:

Door & Hardware Schedule		
Location	Door Style	Hardware
Entrance	Jeld-Wen Prehung Solid Core Molded 6-Panel 2'6"	Stanley Hardware Square Privacy Mortise Bolt
Living Room to Study	Jeld-Wen Pocket Solid Core Molded Smooth 2'6"	Stanley Hardware Rectangular Flush Pull
Closet	Jeld Wen Prehung Solid Core Molded 6-Panel 2'	Stanley Hardware Square Privacy Mortise Bolt

Notes:

Chapter 14
Commands – Set 7: Creating Curves and Rendering

ELEVATION B

SCALE: 1/ 4" = 1'

Learning Objectives:

- Creating curved shapes using Arc, Polyline, and Spline
- Creating an Ellipse
- Using Hatch for sections and to fill shapes and Section Views
- Using Gradient Hatch to render your drawing

Up to this point, we have focused primarily on straight-line shapes. This covers the majority of items we will draw: walls, doors, windows, etc. There are many times that we will need to draw curved shapes. This is especially true for items such as curtains, bedding, upholstery, etc.

Although AutoCAD® is a drafting program, not a drawing program, it has the ability to draw curved shapes. This will take some practice, but once you get used to it, it is easy to do.

Arc

The Arc command creates an arc. There are multiple ways to create an arc. We have used the Circle command with trimming in the previous chapters. Although that may not have been the most efficient method, it was intuitive and straightforward. This section will only cover one method of creating arcs. It is left to the student to explore other methods.

The method covered here is the 3-point arc. This is an arc that is created by picking 3 points. The arc created will have the first and last point picked as the endpoints. The second point picked will define the amount of curvature the arc will have. This type of arc comes in handy when you are working a design where you want to have a curvature bounded by a fixed distance.

Procedure:

Pick (left click): **Arc icon** from the Draw Panel of the Home Tab.

The command line prompts you with the following:

*ARC Specify start point of arc or [Center]**(Pick the first endpoint of the arc – Point "A")***
Specify second point of arc or [Center/End]: ***(Pick the second point which defines the curvature –***
Point "B")
Specify end point of arc: ***(Pick the third point which is the endpoint of the arc – Point "C")***

Once the arc is created, AutoCAD® automatically ends the command.

Try it:

As an example, let's draw an arc that is the shape for the top of a cabinet door. Before beginning, make sure that you have the Object Snap turned on with Endpoint and Midpoint selected.

This is the cabinet door before the arc is created:

To create an arc that curves within a 1″ distance from the bottom of the top frame, let's first Explode the top rectangle (if you had created it as a rectangle).

Use the Offset command and offset the bottom line of the top frame up 1″.

(Pick the Arc icon)

ARC *Specify start point of arc or [Center]:* **(Pick endpoint 1)**
Specify second point of arc or [Center/End]: **(Pick the midpoint of the offset line)**
Specify end point of arc: **(Pick endpoint 2)**

The command is completed and an arc is drawn. Use the Erase command to eliminate the offsite line.

When you are done, the cabinet door will look like this:

Ellipse

The Ellipse command creates an ellipse. An ellipse looks similar to an oval, but it is a unique shape. An elliptical shape is how an object with a circular shape appears when it is viewed at an angle. Sometimes the elliptical shape is used for a table, a mirror, or as an architectural feature such as windows or archways.
An ellipse can be created in multiple ways. It is defined with a major and a minor axis. The default method of creating an ellipse using the icon is to define the two end points of the first axis plus the distance for the second axis.

Prior to creating the ellipse, it is easier to define the boundary of the ellipse by using a rectangle. Make sure the size of the rectangle is the size that you want the ellipse to be. In addition, make sure you have your object snap setting to Midpoint.

Example:

Let's draw the elliptical shape of the coffee table shown:

First, start with a rectangle that is the same dimensions as those shown for the ellipse:

Procedure:

Pick (left click): **Ellipse icon fly-out** from the Draw Panel of the Home Tab. Pick **Axis, End icon.**

The command line prompts you with the following:

ELLIPSE *Specify axis endpoint of ellipse or [Arc/Center]:* **(Pick the midpoint of the first line)**

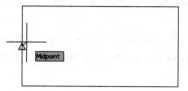

Specify other endpoint of axis: **(Pick the midpoint of the line opposite the first line)**

Specify distance to other axis or [Rotation]: **(Pick the midpoint of either of the two remaining lines)**

Once the ellipse is drawn, use the Erase command to erase the rectangle. The result will be an ellipse to the exact dimensions as shown:

Polyline

Another command that allows you more freedom to draw curved shapes is Polyline. This command allows you to draw straight lines and arcs in a free form (as well as with precision).

For fun, let's draw a heart shape. Let's do this in a free form without worry of a specific size, and we can approximate the shape. Note, however, that the heart shape is symmetrical. We can take advantage of that fact by drawing only half the heart shape and then mirroring that about the line of symmetry.

First, draw the vertical line that we will use to mirror about. Use the construction line, with vertical as the option, to draw a vertical line somewhere on the screen. Once that is done, we can draw the shape of the half-heart. It is recommended that you turn off Object Snap so that you have better control. We will intentionally draw the half-heart crossing the construction line.

Polyline:

The Polyline command is located on the Draw Panel of the Home Tab.

Polyline icon

Procedure:

Pick (left click): **Polyline icon** from the Draw Panel of the Home Tab.

The command line prompts you with the following:

PLINE Specify start point: **(Pick a location on the left side of the vertical construction line)**

Vertical
Construction Line

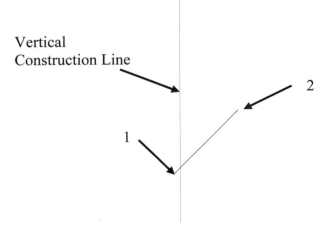

The polyline will rubber-band to follow your cursor. As you pick the second point, the polyline will be a point-to-point line.

Current line-width is 0'-0"
Specify next point or [Arc/Halfwidth/Length/Undo/Width]: **(Pick the second point, up and to the right of the first point)**

Specify next point or [Arc/Close/Halfwidth/Length/Undo/Width]: **a ⏎**

An arc will begin to be drawn. The radius and endpoint will change as it rubber-bands with your cursor movement.

Specify endpoint of arc or
[Angle/CEnter/CLose/Direction/Halfwidth/Line/Radius/Second pt/Undo/Width]: **(Pick a location on the opposite side of the construction line to form the rounded part of the half-heart)**

Specify endpoint of arc or
[Angle/CEnter/CLose/Direction/Halfwidth/Line/Radius/Second pt/Undo/Width]: ⏎

Pressing the ⏎ Enter key will exit the command.

Use the Trim command to trim the half-heart to the Construction Line.

Use the Mirror command to mirror and copy the half-heart shape to become a complete heart shape. Erase the vertical construction line.

Try using the Polyline for any other shapes you would like. If you want to change its shape, use the grips. For multiple hearts, try the Array command. Have fun with it!

Spline

Another command that comes in handy for free-form drawing is the Spline command. The spline is drawn by picking multiple points on the drawing. As you pick those points, the shape will rubber-band with your cursor. To end the command, press the ↵ Enter key

There are two types of splines available: Fit and CV. This chapter will only discuss the Fit version. The Spline commands are located on the Draw Panel of the Home Tab.

Spline Fit
icon

Procedure:

Pick (left click): **Spline Fit icon** from the Draw Panel of the Home Tab.

The command line prompts you with the following:

Current settings: Method=Fit   Knots=Chord
SPLINE *Specify first point or [Method/Knots/Object]:* **(Pick a point on the screen)**
Enter next point or [start Tangency/toLerance]: **(Pick a point on the screen)**
Enter next point or [end Tangency/toLerance/Undo]: **(Pick a point on the screen)**
Enter next point or [end Tangency/toLerance/Undo/Close]: **(Pick a point on the screen)**
Enter next point or [end Tangency/toLerance/Undo/Close]: **(Pick a point on the screen)**
Enter next point or [end Tangency/toLerance/Undo/Close]: ↵

Pressing the ↵ Enter key will exit the command.

Resulting Spline shape

Try it:

As an example, let's draw a spiral shape with horizontal line:

The spiral shape is drawn using the Spline command. It could be done free-hand, or for more control, by using a technique of concentric circles and lines clocked around the circle to define the points of the spline.

Before beginning, ensure that Object Snap is turned on with Center and Intersection options selected.

Draw a 1/8" radius circle and offset it by 1/8", toward the outside, 11 times. The largest circle will be 1-1/2" radius.

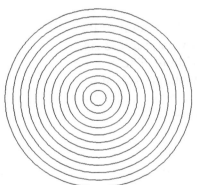

> Concentric circles 1/8"
> apart. Smallest radius
> is 1/8" and the largest
> radius is 1-1/2"

Draw a vertical line from the center of the circles to the top quadrant of the largest circle. You may need to use the Object Snap override of Snap to Quadrant from the Object Snap toolbar.
Use the Polar Array command to rotate and copy the line 8 times within 360°.

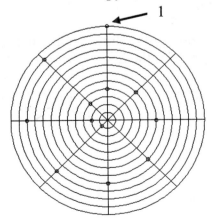

Starting at point 1, use the Spline command and pick the points of intersection of the lines and circles so that each point gets progressively closer to the center.

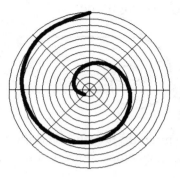

This spline was drawn at a thicker lineweight than the circles and lines to make it easier to distinguish it.

Now that the spline is drawn, you can erase the circles and lines. An easy way to do that is to move the spline to a different location and then use a selection window to erase.

The next thing we want is a line that is tangent to the spline. Use the Line command with Snap to Tangent as an Object Snap override.

Pick the first point of the line above and to the right of the spline. The second point of the line should snap to the tangent point of the spline.

Use the Trim command to trim any excess portion of the spline.

We do not know the angle of the line, but we want to control the line and spiral orientation. For this example, we will rotate the spline and line together so that the line is horizLontal. We will use the Reference option of the Rotate command.

In order to use the Reference option, we will need to draw a horizontal line through the endpoint of the angled line first. It may be necessary to trim the line so that you will have an endpoint to select.

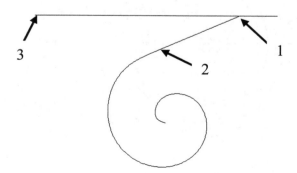

Use the Rotate command to rotate the spline and the line.

Current positive angle in UCS: ANGDIR=counterclockwise ANGBASE=0
ROTATE *Select objects:* **(Pick the spline and line you want to rotate)**
Specify opposite corner: 2 found

Select objects: ↵
Specify base point: **(Pick point 1)**
Specify rotation angle or [Copy/Reference] <0>: **r**↵
Specify the reference angle <0>: **(Pick point 1)** *Specify second point:* **(Pick point 2)**
Specify the new angle or [Points] <0>: **(Pick point 3)**

The spline and line have now rotated so that the line is horizontal.

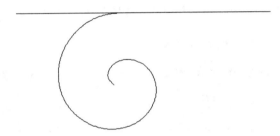

Erase the extra line that we created to use as a reference for rotation. Since this was some amount of work to create this shape, it would be a good idea to save it as a Block for future use.

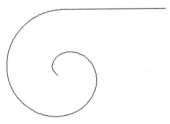

You can try different size circles and different number of lines to pick the intersections and you will get different shaped spirals.

Spiral created using 12 lines   Spiral created using 1/16" offset circles

Hatch

Hatch is used to fill an enclosed area with either a pattern or a solid color. It can be most useful for section views or for the solid fill color of walls for a plan view.

Procedure:

Pick (left click): **Hatch icon** from the Draw Panel of the Home Tab.

The Hatch Creation Tab will appear on the ribbon:

Various patterns or solid colors are available. In addition, a two-color gradient style hatch is also available. User defined is also available, but that will not be covered in this text.

Prior to selecting the enclosed area to fill with a Hatch, choose the type you want by using the pull-down selection the Properties Panel.

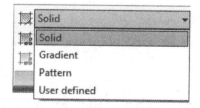

Once you choose the type, a preview of the pattern is highlighted on the Pattern Panel. You can change the pattern by expanding the Pattern Panel.

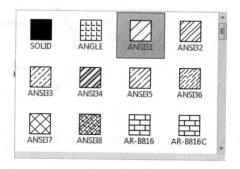

Use the slide bar to preview more hatch patterns.

You can also choose the color of your hatch pattern. Choose the color you want by using the pull-down selection on right side of the Properties Panel. If you pick Select Colors… the Select Color dialog box will appear. This will provide the same color options available to you as when choosing a color for Layers or when using the Properties tool.

Define the boundaries of the hatch by either picking a point in the bounded area or by selecting objects that define the boundary. Using the Pick Points method is preferred but requires the boundary to be completely closed.

Using the Annotative option is similar to using Annotative Text and Dimensions – The scale of the Hatch pattern will coordinate with the scale of the Paper. Use Match Properties to copy the hatch pattern of existing hatch.

Example:

Let's use a solid color Hatch to fill in the walls of the conference room:

Choose Solid by using the pull-down arrow on the Properties Panel of the Hatch Creation Tab:

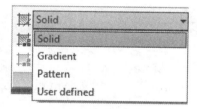

The Solid preview is highlighted in the Pattern Panel of the Hatch Creation Tab:

Use the pull-down arrow for the Hatch Color and choose ByLayer. The color of the Hatch will be the same color as the Layer that it is created in.

Choose the Pick Points button on the Boundaries Panel of the Hatch Creation Tab to select the area that will define the Hatch boundary.

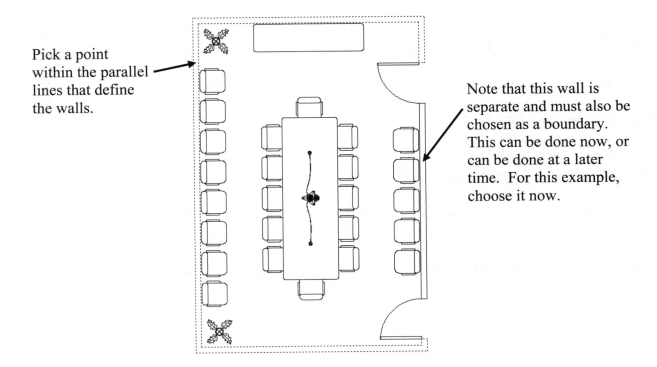

Pick a point within the parallel lines that define the walls.

Note that this wall is separate and must also be chosen as a boundary. This can be done now, or can be done at a later time. For this example, choose it now.

Your command line will display the following:

HATCH Pick internal point or [Select objects/seTtings]:
(Pick a point within the walls to define the boundary)

> Note: Be patient while AutoCAD searches for the boundary. At first, it may not appear that anything happened after you picked a point.

If the boundary is not well defined, or not completely displayed on your screen while you are selecting it, the following error message will appear:

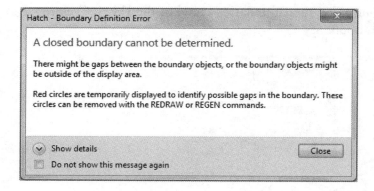

If you get this error message, try to fix the problem via one of the suggested methods given in the error message under the Show details pull-down.

If there are no issues with the boundary, the command line will display the following:

Selecting everything visible...
Analyzing the selected data...
Analyzing internal islands...
Pick internal point or [Select objects/seTtings]:

Since the walls are well defined (no gaps where endpoints of each line should connect) the boundary is displayed with dotted lines. AutoCAD® allows you to define additional boundaries.

Choose a point within the right wall as well. Press the ↵ Enter Key. Your Hatch will appear on your drawing while you select the boundaries.

Press the ↵ Enter Key to accept the Hatch pattern. This will end the command.

Section Views

You can use Hatch for section views. The following is an example of a section view showing a detail of wall cabinets and moulding interface with the ceiling:

MOULDING DETAIL

In this example, the hatch pattern selected was ANSI 31. The angle of the pattern alternated between 0° and 90°.

The trick to making the detail have a "3D" look is to use the true cross-section shape of the moulding and adding 30° angled lines to it. Copy the cross-section shape to the opposite end of the angled lines and it becomes a faked 3D view.

Although the faked 3D view is not technically accurate, it helps provide a very good visual to both the client and the carpenter to be able to understand how things go together.

Rendering

You can use Hatch to render your 2-D drawings. You can accomplish this by using the Gradient Hatch. Unfortunately, Gradient Hatch is not available for the AutoCAD® LT version.

Gradient Hatch

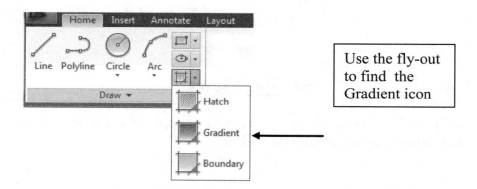

Use the fly-out to find the Gradient icon

Pick (left click): **Gradient icon** from the Draw Panel of the Home Tab.

Note that you can also get to this using the Hatch icon and then selecting Gradient using the pull-down arrow for Hatch Type on the Properties Panel of the Hatch Creation Tab.

The Panel on the Hatch Creation Tab will change to provide gradient tools:

The various styles available can be selected using the pull-down of the Pattern Panel and are shown below (the full names are shown in the text box):

GR_LINEAR	GR_CYLIN	GR_INVCYL
GR_SPHER	GR_HEMISP	GR_CURVED	GR_INVSPH
GR_INVHEM	GR_INVCUR	

Linear
Cylindrical
Inverted cylindrical
Spherical
Hemispherical
Curved
Inverted spherical
Inverted hemispherical
Inverted curved

Gradient works the same as a solid Hatch except that it has two color choices. This allows you to simulate lighting conditions. To create a good visual rendering of your drawing will take practice and patience. It is likely that you may not be satisfied with the color or style the first time you place the Gradient Hatch on the drawing. This does not mean you need to erase it and try again. Instead, it is better to use the Properties Palette to make the changes once the Gradient Hatch is on the drawing.

Another technique that can be employed is to cover small areas at a time. This is especially true when you want to have different effects for different parts of a piece of furniture or areas of a room.

Example:

Let's render the dresser that we created as homework in Chapter 3.

Notice that there are multiple segments that make up the dresser: knobs, drawer fronts, and vertical/horizontal structure. We can add Gradient Hatch to each portion separately.

The following is an example of adding 90° Cylindrical style Gradient Hatch to all the sections (except the knobs) at once:

If we choose each section individually, using the same style we will obtain the following effects:

If you are not happy with the color or style, you can easily change them by using the Properties Palette. Let's change the vertical legs of the dresser to a linear style with the lighter portion toward the inside. For the left leg, this is a Gradient Angle of 0°, and for the right leg, it is 180°.

After selecting a Gradient Hatch, the Properties Palette will allow you to change various features. The features that are most commonly changed for Gradient Hatch are Color 1, Color 2, Gradient Angle, and Centered.

Another technique that can be applied is to divide up the area that you wish to add the Gradient Hatch. As an example, let's say that you have a lamp next to a wall. The color will be lighter nearest the lamp as a result of the intensity of the light in close proximity to the lamp. Let's explore this with two floor lamps. Each lamp will have an affect on the appearance of the wall color.

Using Cylindrical style for the wall will not provide the effect we are looking for:

Notice that the Cylindrical style would make it appear as though the light was centered on the wall. One way around this problem is to divide the room into sections. We can draw a vertical line from each floor lamp and another centered in the room to divide it into reasonable sections.

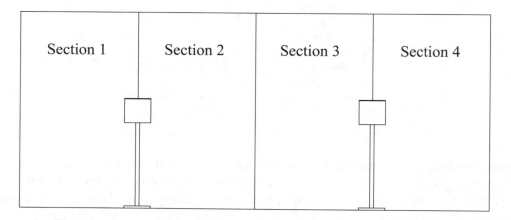

With the room divided into sections, we can add Gradient Hatch to each section. The following shows the result of using Linear style with sections 1 and 3 set at a Gradient Angle of 0° and sections 2 and 4 set at a Gradient Angle of 180°. The lines used to divide the wall have been erased.

It may not produce perfect results, but it certainly provides for a much more realistic appearance.

Summary

In this chapter you have learned to:

- Draw a 3-point Arc
- Create an Ellipse using a rectangle to define the boundaries
- Use a Polyline to draw continuous lines and arcs
- Draw a free-form curve using Spline
- Use Hatch to fill an area with a solid color or other pre-defined patterns
- Render your drawing using Gradient Hatch – Filling an area with two-color solid hatch
- Use various techniques to improve the appearance of your rendered drawing

Review Questions

1. Why would you use an Arc instead of a Circle?

2. How is an Ellipse defined?

3. What situation would you use a Polyline?

4. Why would you use a Spline instead of a Polyline?

5. If your Hatch does not appear the right size, what can you do about it?

6. What can you do if you get an error message while trying to insert Hatch?

7. How is Gradient different than Hatch?

8. How many different styles of Gradient Hatch are there available?

9. If you are not satisfied with the Gradient Hatch you put in, how can you change it without re-creating it?

10. For Gradient Hatch for a locally lit area, what technique can you use to get an improved appearance?

Exercises

1. Add to the drawing that you created through Tutorial 5 by using solid Hatch for the walls in the Plan View. Choose whichever color you desire. In addition, edit the view symbol to add solid hatch and add a view symbol for Elevation B. Change the coffee table from a rectangular shape to an elliptical shape.

2. Download the Hotel Suite Living Room Elevation Blocks from the publisher's web site. Create Elevation B from the Plan View. Create a Layout tab for Elevation B. Set and lock the scale to a standard scale value. Complete the titleblock and annotate your drawing as desired.

3. Create the Radiator Cover. Use NET3 style Hatch with a scale of 6 for the screen. Use a 3-point arc to create the curved top of each side.

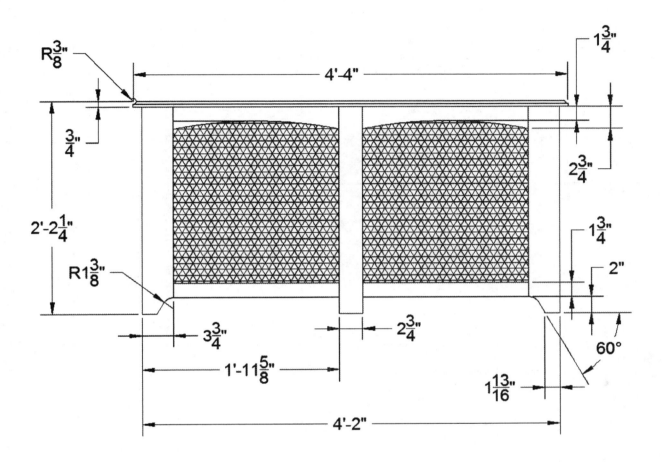

4. Create the cross-section of the radiator cover. Use Hatch and annotate your drawing as shown.

5. Create the wrought iron wall hanging. Use either Polyline or Spline to create one of the shaped ends. Use the Mirror command as well as the Array command to complete the design.

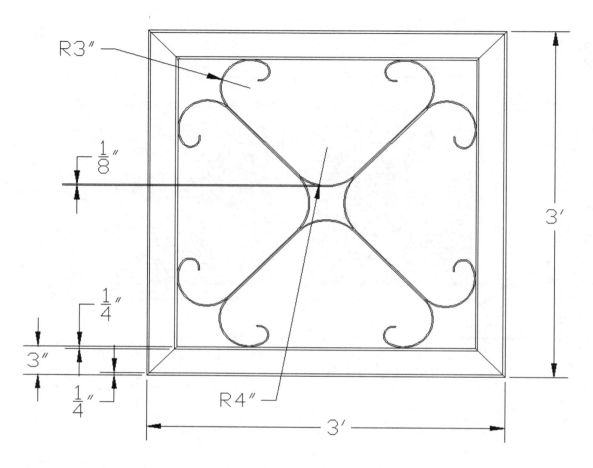

6. Render Elevation B by using both Hatch and Gradient Hatch.

7. Create the moulding detail that was shown as an example in this chapter.

MOULDING DETAIL

The cabinet frame is 3/4" x 2" with 1/2" plywood top (each ply is drawn 1/8" thick). The Blocking is 3/4" x 3/4". Use the following dimensions for the crown moulding, and the base moulding:

To create the appearance of 3D, draw 30° angled lines (use construction lines with angle -30°). Trim the construction lines a reasonable distance away. Copy the profile of the moulding to opposite end of the construction line. Trim the remaining lines as needed.

Notes:

Chapter 15
Miscellaneous – Techniques, Commands, and Options

Learning Objectives:

- **Improve drawing techniques**
- **Use several new commands**
- **Explore additional command options**
- **Trace objects and correct the scale**

Up to this point, we have learned enough of the AutoCAD® program to be able to be productive and create our interior designs. This chapter provides some review of what we already know and consolidates them into helpful hints. In addition, there are some occasionally used commands that are explored, as well as some additional options for commands we have already learned. For the most part, you could get by without knowing the commands and options covered in this chapter and you would still be very productive. However, it is certainly worth exploring these since they can come in handy.

Helpful Hints

The following helpful hints summarize what you already know.

1. When you first begin a new drawing, make sure the units are properly set.

2. As you are about to start drawing, look at what you need to draw with an eye toward the best approach to drawing. Ask yourself if you should use lines, rectangles or construction lines.

3. AutoCAD® offers multiple ways of doing the same thing. Icons, pull down menus, typing commands, and shortcuts are available. At first this can be confusing and overwhelming. Please do not let this discourage you. Use whichever method you are most comfortable with.

4. Try not to get overwhelmed by the X-Y coordinate system. Try to avoid it by using Construction Lines instead of Lines. Use the Line command when there are two specific points to snap the end points. Use the Offset and Trim commands to clean up the Construction Lines. The extra steps will go faster with more practice. In fact, you will likely get so fast that thinking of the exact X-Y value would take twice as long.

5. Any time you need to start a line or other geometry a specific distance away from another line, use the Offset command (or Construction Line/Offset) to find an intersection point. Use the Object Snap/Intersection setting to find your start point. After you are done, simply erase the construction line. This can also be done by using Circles for construction purposes and erasing them when you are done.

6. I find the Grid/Snap to be a hindrance; I do not use them, and did not cover it in this text. Instead, I make extensive use of Object Snaps.

7. Use the Fillet command with a radius of zero to trim/extend lines simultaneously, such as a corner for an outside line for a wall.

8. When using a fly-out style icon, such as Measure Geometry (Distance), remember that the icon displayed was the last one used. So if the last measurement made was Angle, and now you want to measure a Distance, move the cursor over the Angle fly-out icon, press and <u>hold</u>

the left mouse button. The remaining icons "fly-out". While still holding the left mouse button, move your cursor down to the Distance icon and then release the left mouse button.

9. An alternate method of moving around the drawing instead of the Zoom and Pan commands is to use the wheel on the mouse. Rolling the wheel forward and backward will Zoom in and out of the drawing. Pressing the wheel down and dragging will allow you to Pan around your drawing. For zooming the entire drawing, double-click the mouse wheel.

Finding the Center of a Rectangle

There are times when you need to locate the center of a rectangle. As an example, if you are creating a reflected ceiling plan, you may want to locate a fixture in the middle of the room. If you have a rectangular room, it is easy to find the center.

If you were drawing this by hand, you would likely draw two diagonal lines from corner to opposite corner to form an "X". The intersection of the lines would be the exact center of the rectangle.

With AutoCAD®, you do not need to draw two lines. You can take advantage of the Snap to Midpoint feature and just draw one line between opposite corners. Of course, when you are done, simply erase the diagonal line.

Divide

There are times when it is desired to divide an object into equal segments. Typically, this would be a line or a circle. However, AutoCAD® will allow you to divide other objects as well. AutoCAD® will divide the object in equal perimeter true distance.

Before using the Divide command, set the Point Style. To set the Point Style, use the pull-down arrow to expand the Utilities Panel of the Home Tab and select Point Style. The Point Style dialog box appears. Choose a style, set the desired size, and then pick OK.

Procedure:

Type: **div**⏎ in the command line

The command line prompts you with the following:

DIVIDE *Select object to divide:* **(Pick the object that you want to divide)**
Enter the number of segments or [Block]: **Type a number and then press the** ⏎ **Enter key**

AutoCAD® ends the command.

In order to snap to a point, set Snap to Node on. AutoCAD® refers to points as nodes.

Try it:

After you set the Point Style using the Format pull-down menu, draw a line that is arbitrarily long at any angle on your screen:

Use the Divide command to divide the line into 5 equal segments. When you are done, your drawing will look like this:

Let's draw vertical construction lines through the points that were just created. Make sure Snap to Node is selected in the Object Snap setting. Now use the Construction Line icon and choose the Vertical option. Pick each point for the vertical construction line to snap to. When you are done, your drawing will look like this:

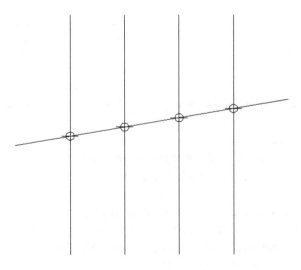

Break & Break at Point

There are times when it is desired to split a line, arc, etc. into two segments. This can be accomplished by using either the Break command or the Break at Point command. These are both located on the Modify Panel of the Home Tab.

Break icon

Break at Point icon

The Break command will break the object into two segments and trim away a portion of the object that you selected. The amount that is trimmed away is dependent on where the object was selected and the location picked for the break point.

Let's use a line as an example of the Break command.

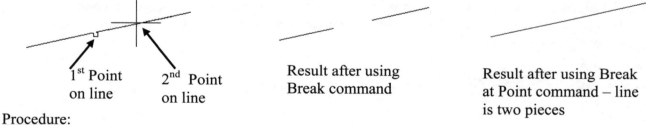

1st Point on line

2nd Point on line

Result after using Break command

Result after using Break at Point command – line is two pieces

Procedure:

Pick (left click): **Break icon** [or **Break at Point icon**] from the Modify toolbar.

*BREAK Select object: (**Pick the line**)*
*Specify second break point or [First point]: (**Pick a point on the line**)*
AutoCAD® ends the command.

The Break at Point command is the same as the Break command except AutoCAD automatically selects the First point option for you. This option means that the first point selected for the break will be defined by picking a location rather than the location at which the object was selected. The second point selected will automatically be chosen as the first point. The break will not be obvious because no gap will be shown.

<u>Stretch</u>

You can change the shape of an object by using the Stretch command. You can make several objects longer or shorter in one direction. An example would be if you wanted to modify the size of a room. This could be handled using the Move command and then trimming/extending the remaining objects to match. You need to exercise caution when using stretch because the objects could easily become distorted. It is important to have set up the base and target points to stretch from and to. The icon is on the Modify Panel of the Home Tab.

<u>Example:</u>

Below is an 8′ x 10′ room. The client desires to change the 8′ direction to 12′.

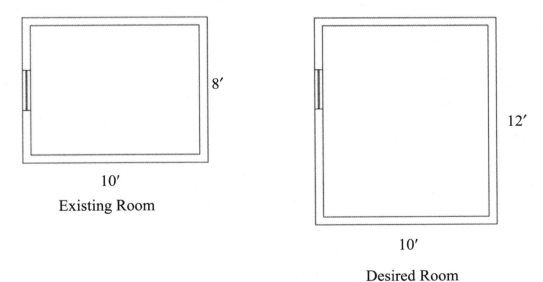

Existing Room

Desired Room

In order to use the Stretch command, offset the top horizontal line 4′ down. This will allow us to use Snap to Endpoint for the base and target points.

Offset this line
down 4' down

Procedure:

Pick (left click): **Stretch icon** from the Modify Panel of the Home Tab.

STRETCH *Select Objects:*
Use a crossing window to select the 4 vertical lines and the bottom horizontal lines:

Point 1

Point 2

Since no more objects are to be selected, press the ↵ Enter key. This will bring us to the second part of the command.

Specify base point or [Displacement] <Displacement>: **(Pick Point 1)**
Specify second point or <use first point as displacement>: **(Pick Point 2)**

The result of the Stretch command looks like this:

Without good base and target points, the room could end up distorted:

It is because of this that you need to exercise caution and set things up first to avoid having this happen.

Scale

The Scale command allows you to change the size of the selected object in both directions. The object can either be enlarged or reduced depending on the scale factor you key in. If the scale factor is greater than 1, the object will be enlarged. If it is less than 1, it will be reduced.

Example:

Let's enlarge a 1′ radius circle. We want the circle to be twice as big as it is, so the scale factor will be 2.

Procedure:

Pick (left click): **Scale icon** from the Modify toolbar.

*SCALE Select objects: **(Pick the circle)** 1 found*
Select objects: ↵
*Specify base point: **(Pick the center of the circle)***
Specify scale factor or [Copy/Reference]: **2**↵

The result is a circle with a 2′ radius (2 x 1′ = 2′)

Calculate Scale Factor

Determining the correct scale factor may require the use of a calculator. To determine what the scale factor is that you need, remember the following guideline:

> **Scale Factor = (What you want) ÷ (What you have)**

Example 1: An object measures 10" and you want it to be 15"; the scale factor is 1.5:

What you want = 15; What you have = 10; Then the Scale Factor = 15 ÷ 10 = 1.5

This may have been easy enough for some people to do the math in their head. Sometimes, the factor can become cumbersome to calculate.

Example 2: An object measures 3' 2-5/16" and you want it to be 4'; the scale factor is 1.25285481:

Scale Factor = 4' ÷ 3' 2-5/16" = 1.25285481

Example 3: An object measures 3' 2-5/16" and you want it to be 3'; the scale factor is 0.939641109:

Scale Factor = 3' ÷ 3' 2-5/16" = 0.939641109

Fortunately, AutoCAD® has a calculator available that can assist you.

QuickCalc:

The QuickCalc icon can be found on the Utilities Panel of the Home Tab.

When you select the icon, the QuickCalc palette becomes available:

There are several features available in the QuickCalc palette. We will only explore the Basic Calculator Mode.

> Prior to using QuickCalc, it is best to change your units back to decimal to get a more accurate scale factor.

<u>Example:</u>

Change the size of the square to 3′x3′. This is the "What you want" part of the scale factor calculation. From the picture shown, "What you have" is 2′5-1/4".

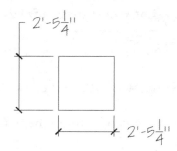

Pick the QuickCalc icon to make it available. Expand the Application Menu Browser and use the Drawing Utilities to change the drawing units from Architectural to Decimal.

To find the scale factor, the calculation we plan to use is (3′) ÷ (2′5-1/4"). Since we have changed the drawing units to decimal, we cannot use architectural units in the calculation. Use either 3 x12 or 36 for the 3′ measurement, since decimal units are in inches only.

Enter the "What you want" value in the QuickCalc display area followed by the "/" (divide) function.

Pick the Distance icon in the QuickCalc calculator. The calculator will disappear from the display and the command line will prompt you to pick two points to measure the distance between. Pick two endpoints of a horizontal line. The calculator will re-appear on the screen with the measured value in the display. This is the "What you have" value. Pick the "=" (equal) function to complete the calculation.

We now have the scale factor we need to change the size of the square.

Pick the Scale command and select the square.

SCALE Select objects: **(Pick the square)** *1 found*
Select objects: ↵
Specify base point: **(Pick one of the corner points of the square)**
Specify scale factor or [Copy/Reference]: **(Pick the Paste Value icon from QuickCalc)** *1.23076923*↵

The square has now changed to the size that you want.

Remember to change your units back to Architectural before continuing work on your drawing.

Cut (or Copy)/Paste – Using the Clipboard

Changing Objects from Model Space to Paper Space

You can easily move an object that you created in Model Space to Paper Space by using a cutting and pasting technique. For example, let's say you have created the Titleblock, in Model Space, shown below:

In order to get it out of model space and into paper space, use the following instructions:

Procedure:

1. Pick the Cut icon from the Clipboard Panel of the Home Tab. Use a Selection Window (or a Crossing Window) to select all the objects. Press the ↵ Enter key.

Step 2 ⟶   ⟵ Step 1

2. Pick one of the Layout tabs.

3. Pick the Paste icon from the Clipboard Panel of the Home Tab.

4. An image of the Titleblock will follow your cursor. Pick on the screen to finish pasting the Titleblock in Paper Space.

Now that the Titleblock is a Paper Space object, use the Move command to re-locate it on your layout.

This same cut/paste or copy/paste technique can also be used when you want objects from another drawing that are not already defined as blocks to be brought in to your drawing. You must have both drawings open and use the pull-down Window (at the top of your screen) to switch between drawings. Use the Switch Windows icon on the User Interface Panel of the View Tab to toggle between open drawings.

Tracing Pictures

There are times when certain pieces of furniture, such as upholstered furniture, would be needed on your drawing. Since these typically have many curves, it is difficult to simply measure and draw using lines and trimming, etc.

One technique that can be used is to cut/paste a digital picture into the AutoCAD® drawing screen. You can use a photograph of the furniture or you could cut a picture from an internet catalog. It is best to get a picture looking straight on the furniture instead of at an angle.

The following example uses a picture of a sofa cut from the internet:

Procedure:

1. Find a picture on the internet that you want to trace. For this example, we will use the sofa.
2. Right-click on the picture in the advertisement and select Copy image.

This will copy the picture of the sofa onto the clipboard.

3. Switch from the internet browser to AutoCAD®.
4. Use the Paste icon from the Clipboard Panel of the Home Tab.
5. A rectangular shape will follow your cursor. Pick a location on the drawing screen to paste the picture into your drawing. The image of the sofa, with a rectangle outlining the boundary of the image, will appear.

Now that we have an image of the sofa on our drawing, we can trace it. It is a good idea to create a new layer for our tracing so that we can turn the image on and off to monitor our tracing progress. In addition, we can also use a contrasting color and a thick lineweight.

Let's start with some easy shapes to trace first, such as straight-lines sections like the legs.

6. Use the Zoom command to zoom in on a leg. Pick the Line command and insert lines to trace the shape of the leg.

A contrasting color, thick line is used to trace the outline of the leg. Zoom in to get as close as possible for a more accurate trace. Use the wheel mouse to zoom in and out and pan to different locations.

Continue tracing the straight-line sections in a similar manner. For the curved shapes, we can use splines.

7. Zoom in on a curved shape and pick the Spline command to insert a spline.

Continue tracing the curved shapes in a similar manner. For certain curves that are meant to be arcs, you can use the Circle or Arc commands instead of the Spline command. An arc may be most appropriate to use for the back of the sofa. It is your choice.

8. Turn off the layer that had the image pasted to it. What remains is the tracing that you just completed. If you notice any areas you may have missed, you can turn the layer back on and finish the tracing. Be sure to turn the image layer back off when done making corrections.

When you are done, your drawing will look like this:

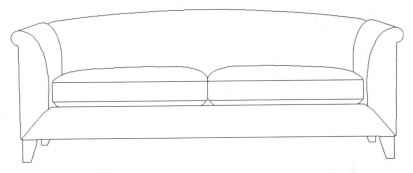

As a pictorial representation of the sofa, the tracing looks great! However, since we are very concerned about proper size, we will need to adjust the size of the tracing using the Scale command.

Measure the height and width of the sofa and compare those dimensions to the advertised size. The advertised dimensions for this sofa are 80"W x 35" H.

The measured values for our tracing is not what we want. It will vary depending on how large the image was when you pasted it to your drawing. My measurements are 154'11-3/8" W x 62'3-11/16"H:

9. To correct for the width, use the Scale command and the QuickCalc method described earlier in this chapter. In this case, the scale factor is 0.0430247228. (80/1859.39606)

After we scale this, the new dimensions are now 80"W x 32-3/16"H. It does not measure to the exact height we wanted because the picture was taken at a slight angle.

To correct for the 2-13/16" height difference, we need to be a little creative. We can use the Stretch command and change the height in sections that will not be too noticeable. We can share the distance in a two areas by making the cushions a little thicker and the legs a little longer. If we make the legs 1-1/4" longer, then we would need to make the cushions 1-9/16" thicker (2-13/16" - 1-1/4" = 1-9/16"). Let's try this combination and see what the results look like.

10. Draw a vertical and horizontal construction line on the drawing. These can be anywhere on your drawing. Offset the horizontal construction line 1-14". We will use the intersections for our stretch distance and direction.

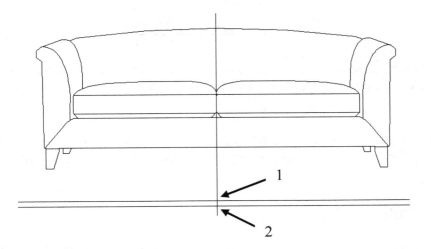

11. Pick the Stretch command and use a Crossing Window to select the legs. Pick intersection 1 as the Base "from" point and location 2 as the "to" point.
12. Erase one of the horizontal construction lines. Offset the remaining horizontal construction line 1-9/16".
13. Pick the Stretch command and use a Crossing Window to select the lower section of the sofa thru the mid-section of the cushions. Pick intersection 1 as the Base "from" point and location 2 as the "to" point.

When we are done, the sofa will now be the correct dimensions. The increased leg and cushion heights are not too noticeable. If you don't like the look of thicker cushions, try stretching other portions instead. The key is to get the correct height and be satisfied with the look.

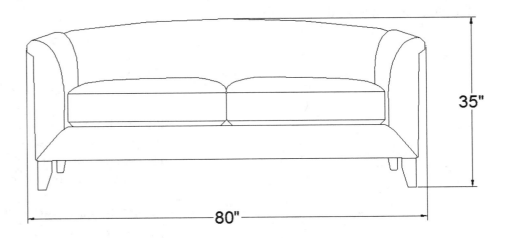

Circle Options

In Chapter 2, we learned the basic concept of the Circle command. We were able to define the circle by specifying the center point and either the radius or diameter. This is not the only way to create a circle.

AutoCAD® offers many options of specifying a circle. These options are shown in the square brackets of the Circle command prompt: *[3P/2P/Ttr (tan tan radius)]*. The following describes each of those options.

Define the Circle with 3 points

This option allows you to define a circle using 3 points that lie on the circumference of the circle.

To use this option after selecting the Circle icon, type **3p↵**

CIRCLE Specify center point for circle or [3P/2P/Ttr (tan tan radius)]: **3p↵**

The command line prompts you to specify the points on the circle:

Specify first point on circle: **(Pick a point on the screen)**
Specify second point on circle: **(Pick a point on the screen)**
Specify third point on circle: **(Pick a point on the screen)**

This can come in very handy for a situation where you want a circle (or an arc after trimming the circle) to be between 3 lines and you don't know (or care) what the diameter of the circle will be. Use Snap to Tangent as you pick each of the three lines.

Example:

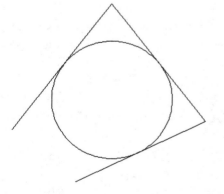

Using the 3 point option for creating a circle comes in handy when you want a circle to be nested between three lines. You must use Snap to Tangent when selecting the lines.

Define the Circle with 2 points

This option allows you to define a circle by using 2 points that define the endpoints of the diameter of the circle.

To use this option after selecting the Circle icon, type **2p↵**

CIRCLE Specify center point for circle or [3P/2P/Ttr (tan tan radius)]: **2p↵**

The command line prompts you to specify the points on the circle:

Specify first end point of circle's diameter: **(Pick a point on the screen)**
Specify second end point of circle's diameter: **(Pick a point on the screen)**

This could be useful in a situation such as drawing piping on an upholstered chair or a full bullnose for the edge of a countertop. After drawing the circle, it can be trimmed and you would now have a semi-circle.

Example:

2 point circle drawn using the endpoints of two parallel lines

The same 2 point circle can be trimmed resulting in a semi-circle

Tan Tan Radius

This option allows you to define a circle that is tangent to two objects of a specific radius. The two objects can be circles, arcs, lines, or combinations of two of these object types. The radius specified must be large enough to be tangent to the two objects.

To use this option you must already have two objects that you plan to have the circle be tangent to. After selecting the Circle icon, type **t↵**

CIRCLE Specify center point for circle or [3P/2P/Ttr (tan tan radius)]: **t↵**

Specify point on object for first tangent of circle: **(Pick one of the objects)**
Specify point on object for second tangent of circle: **(Pick the second object)**
Specify radius of circle: **1↵**

If the radius that you specify is smaller than is physically possible to also be tangent to the two objects, AutoCAD® will provide you with the following message in the command line and end the Circle command:

Circle does not exist.

This can come in handy when you want to draw circles between two arcs/circles, or lines/circles, etc.

<u>Example:</u>

Varying diameter round objects, such as oranges, in a glass container: These make contact with each other or the container at two points.

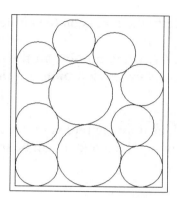

Rectangle Options

In Chapter 3, we learned the basic concept of the Rectangle command. We were able to define the rectangle by specifying one corner point, specifying the distance in both the horizontal and vertical directions, and the location of the opposite corner. This method provided a rectangle with square corners.

Chamfered corner rectangle

Filleted corner rectangle

Chamfered Corner Rectangle

For rectangles with chamfered corners:
Specify first corner point or [Chamfer/Elevation/Fillet/Thickness/Width]:

Type "**c**" and then press the ↵ Enter key.

Specify first chamfer distance for rectangles <X'-X">:

Type in the chamfer value then press the ↵ Enter key.

Specify second chamfer distance for rectangles <X'-X">:

Type in the chamfer value then press the ↵ Enter key. Note that both first and second values should be the same for a 45° chamfer.

After the chamfer values have been keyed in, AutoCAD® prompts for the location of the corner points of the rectangle as described before.

Filleted Corner Rectangle

For rectangles with filleted corners:

Specify fillet radius for rectangles <X'-X">:

Type in the fillet radius value then press the enter key.

After the fillet value has been keyed in, AutoCAD® prompts for the location of the corner points of the rectangle as described before.

Offset Options

In Chapter 3, we learned the basic concept of the Offset command. We were able to offset lines, circles, or rectangles by specifying a distance first, and then selecting the object and direction to offset. This method is most commonly used because you usually know the distance you desire to offset. In some instances, you may wish to offset to a specific location without knowing the distance.

AutoCAD® Calculates Distance

You can specify a distance by picking two points on the drawing. AutoCAD® will automatically calculate the distance between points and will use that value for the offset distance. The points chosen can be any arbitrary points, snapping to grid points, or snapping to specific parts of objects (such as endpoints of a line).

After picking the first point, the command line prompts you with the following:

Specify offset distance or [Through] <X'-XX>: Specify second point:

After you pick the second point the remainder of the prompts are the same as what you learned in Chapter 3.

Pick Object First, then Specify Distance – the Through option

Use this option if you don't know the distance you plan to offset. First, the object is selected, and then the distance is defined by picking in the drawing. Typically, you would choose an end point or intersection, or some specific location for the offset value.

Specify offset distance or [Through/Erase/Layer] <Through>: **t↵**
Select object to offset or <exit>:
Specify through point:
You can select a through point or move your cursor in the direction you want to offset and key in a value for a distance to offset.

AutoCAD® will continue to prompt for more objects to offset:
Select object to offset or <exit>:

To exit the command, press the ↵ Enter key or press the Esc key.

Trim/Extend Options

Edge

Use this choice when the cutting edge (or boundary edge for Extend) does not cross the object to trim/extend, but it would if it was extended. Type **e** in the command line and press the ↵ Enter key for this choice.

> *Select object to trim or shift-select to extend or [Project/Edge/Undo]:* **e↵**

AutoCAD® prompts you with the following:

Enter an implied edge extension mode [Extend/No extend] <No extend>:

For extend mode, type **e** in the command line and press the ↵ Enter key.

> *Enter an implied edge extension mode [Extend/No extend] <No extend>:* **e↵**

Drafting Settings

We have only taken advantage of a few Drafting Setting features: Object Snap and Show/Hide Lineweights. There are other settings that you may have a preference to use. A very brief description of some of these will be given here. Since you already know about Object Snap, that will not be described here. If you are interested in exploring these, or others, any further, the best way is to try them and to also check the Help menu.

Access to Drafting Settings is obtained by using the toggle icons on the left side of the Status Bar.

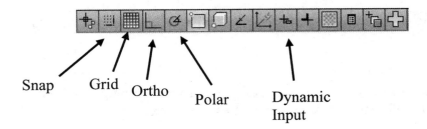

Snap   Grid   Ortho   Polar   Dynamic Input

Changing any settings for any of the drafting features is accomplished by bringing up the Drafting Settings dialog box. This is accomplished by right-clicking on any of the toggle icons and selecting drafting settings:

After right-clicking a toggle icon, select Settings…

There are several tabs across the top of the dialog box. Use these to change settings.

Snap and Grid

You can use a grid and allow your cursor to snap to the grid when you make your drawing. Some people work with this, but I find it more tedious than it is worth. The grid and snap settings are to the nearest increment that you choose. One reason for not using it is because real-world dimensions never fall exactly on a grid. The best way to get familiar with the grid and snap feature is to try it. For further info, it is recommended that you check the Help menu.

Ortho and Polar

Ortho restricts you to horizontal (0°) and vertical (90°) directions only. This could be used on occasion when you prefer to insert a line instead of a construction line for either a horizontal or vertical direction. Otherwise, this has limited use.

Polar is similar to Ortho except it allows you to have more than 0° and 90° increments.

Dynamic Input

The Dynamic Input feature allows you to key in values and provides prompts at the location of the cursor. This is a personal preference whether to have this turned on or not.

Try it:

Draw a 2' x 4' rectangle using the Line command with the Ortho and Polar buttons turned on.

Pick the first point of the line and move the cursor to the right. The line will be drawn and held in a horizontal orientation. The dynamic input will display how long the line is while you are drawing. Simply type 4' followed by the ⏎ Enter key, and it will automatically set the length of the horizontal line to 4'.

Next, move the cursor upward and a second line will be drawn and held in a vertical orientation. Again, the dynamic input will display how long the line is while you are drawing. Simply type 2' followed by the ⏎ Enter key, and it will automatically set the length of the vertical line to 2'.

Continue on this way, but close the last point by selecting the end point of the first line. When you are done, you will have the 2' x 4' rectangle.

Customize User Interface

You may find that the default Panels and Tabs are not efficiently designed for the way you like to do your work. If you like to use the Construction Line command frequently, you may find it cumbersome to not have that command displayed on the top of the Draw Panel. Fortunately, AutoCAD® allows you to customize the workspace.

The Customize User Interface command can be found on the Customization Panel of the Manage tab. It can also be found by expanding the Workspace Switching icon on the lower right of the screen and selecting Customize...

When you pick the CUI tool, the Customize User Interface dialog box will appear. Right-click Workspaces and select New Workspace.

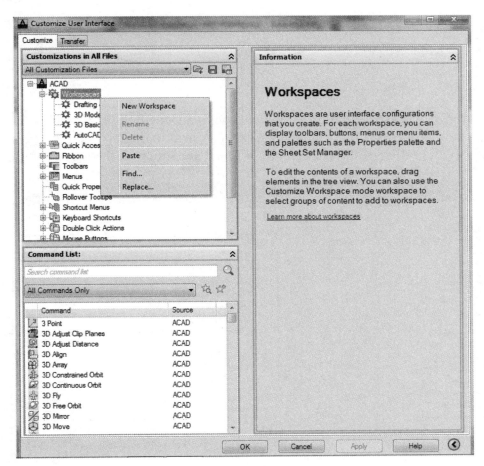

A new Workspace1 will appear, ready for editing. Rename this to Interior Design.

Expand the tree items below Ribbon on the upper left portion of the dialog box. Pick the Customize Workspace button on the upper right portion of the dialog box.

After you pick the Customize Workspace button, it will change to a Done button. Choose which Panels you want for the new Workspace by placing a check-mark next to them. The items you select will appear on the upper right portion of the dialog box. When complete, pick the Done button.

You can change the content of a Panel. Expand Panels from the tree in the upper left portion of the dialog box.

Scroll down the list in the tree to find Home 2-D Draw and select it and expand it. Once you select it, a Panel Preview will appear on the upper right portion of the dialog box.

In the tree on the left portion, there are three rows for the 2-D Draw panel. Expand the first two.

We will move the Construction Line from the second row to the first row above the Line command by picking and dragging. A drag bar will be displayed and will follow your cursor as you move.

After you release the mouse button, the Panel Preview will update. Notice that the icon for Construction Line is small in comparison to the others in the first row. We can change the appearance by using the Properties section in the lower right portion of the dialog box.

We can change the button style of the Construction Line by using the pull-down arrow and selecting Large with Text (vertical).

After you select this style, the Panel Preview will update to show the larger icon for the Construction Line.

As an alternative, you may want to change all the icons to a smaller size without text to save space on your Panel. Make it however you like – this is customizing for your use!

When you are done, be sure to select Apply and OK buttons to close the dialog box.

Now that you have created a new Workspace, you will need to select it to use it. Pick the Workspace Switching icon. Interior Design is now available. Select it and your screen will change to your new customized workspace.

Congratulations! You are now ready to become a valuable and productive AutoCAD® designer.

Notes:

Index